I found this book to be surprisingly enlightening, well-researched, and very easy to read. Mr. Koerner has done his homework, and it shows. He has opened my eyes to data on some of the most controversial questions of our time—data I didn't know existed. The Genesis account of human history has much more historical and scientific evidence than most people—even Christians—are aware of. This is worth the read!

Pastor Chris Francis
True Life Church
chris@truelifenj.com
732-202-7509
tuelifenj.com

Gospel Mission Corps October 23 2023
Fresh Ponds Chapel
27 Old Davidson Mills Rd
South Brunswick, NJ
P.O. Box 361 Dayton NJ 08810
gospelworkers@aol.com
732-297-3008 Christian Faith Publishing

Att. Michael Mongera
I found Exploring the book of Genesis excellent in its enlightenment of the Holy Scriptures and historical research. I learned more than I thought I already knew about the book of Genesis. Thank you, Bob Harty Koerner, for a job well done. I enthusiastically recommend his book to all the body of Christ.

Pastor Richard Swanson

Pastor Richard Swanson

Below is my endorsement for the book written by Bob Harty Koerner, which is written as an exposition of the book of Genesis:

After reviewing the manuscript for this book, I found it to be thought-provoking and well researched. This has been a labor of love for Bob, and I know that his heart desires that this book draw the reader closer to both our Holy God and His Holy Word.

Joseph Turner
October 25, 2023

I have known Bob Harty-Koerner for a few years and have witnessed his dedication to writing *Exploring the Book of Genesis,* along with his strong religious beliefs in God and the Bible, that have brought this book to fruition. Bob's message throughout this book is God's creation and the love of humanity.

This book couldn't have been published at a better time than now, with the upheaval and unrest the world is witnessing today. I would urge all of today's world leaders to read this book.

As stated in the book's preface,

> The Bible is the holy Word of God. His Word is Truth (Jeremiah 29:13–14, 1 Peter 3:15). Early church Father St. Gerome stated that "ignorance of the scripture is ignorance of Christ." In reference to the Holy Bible, Queen Victoria said, "This book is the secret of England's greatness." Abraham Lincoln stated, "I believe the Bible is the best gift God has given to man," and Theodore Roosevelt said, "No educated man can afford to be ignorant of the Bible." We have God's Word. Let's live by it.

Exploring the Book of Genesis is an excellent book and should be read by all walks of life.

Warmest Regards,
Irene Darmetko

October 22, 2023
741 Midstreams Road
Brick, NJ 08724

Exploring THE BOOK OF GENESIS

A Commentary on Origins, Sin, Faith, Salvation, Science and Historical Perspectives

Bob Harty Koerner

ISBN 979-8-88751-057-6 (paperback)
ISBN 979-8-88751-058-3 (digital)

Christian Faith Publishing
832 Park Avenue
Meadville, PA 16335
www.christianfaithpublishing.com

Printed in the United States of America

This book is dedicated to

the Lord Jesus,
the Jewish Messiah

and to

my dear sweetheart,
Mimi

Without her love and patience, this book in its
present form would not have been possible.

CONTENTS

PREFACE

Because of the serious controversy created during debates by renowned scientists over the vitally important issue of creation versus evolution, it is my hope that more and more students and teachers may become interested in the ancient and controversial but powerful, enlightening book of Genesis. Although the majority of students and teachers will believe what they choose to believe and usually accept whatever is taught, I still must stress that it is the duty and responsibility of every student to seek this truth without prejudice or presupposition but with real interest and an open mind. This concise commentary is designed to be a relevant aid to diligent students who desire to achieve a fuller and more rewarding understanding of Genesis. As a longtime history student and Bible scholar, I have discovered the answers to many ancient mysteries located in Genesis; so now it is time to share this amazing and enlightening knowledge with teachers, students, and truth seekers everywhere. This book is not a detailed analysis. Rather, it is an in-depth study made easy to understand. However, this book is intentionally brief to minimize the time to read it, since students are busy people. So it is carefully designed to enhance and thoroughly equip students with vital information that they would normally not be exposed to in other texts.

In order to best understand and truly appreciate this brief but comprehensive book, I recommend that my students must also read the book of Genesis. The spiritual, theological, and historical information can best be understood when both books are carefully and lovingly, with effort, compared to each other or read together. My hopes are that doing so will be a life-changing experience. My desire is to bring many souls to Christ.

The morals of our postmodern society are rapidly changing, so this book will deal with relevant points of interest pertaining to history, creation, sin, faith, trust, mysteries, and salvation. Also, this book was written to be enjoyed, so I recommend that the curious and motivated readers and researchers take notice of the truly unique quality of each chapter and paragraph.

It will appear to some teachers that I intentionally use more than one genre or writing style throughout this treatise or text. But each subject is different in structure, and each unique chapter of Genesis is of an unusual and changing nature. The student will discover many differences contained in the treatise, demonstrating that within this text, each chapter is by itself a book within this book.

This fascinating and informative history book was originally much smaller and started out as a Bible college term paper. With a great deal of work and much comparative research, I have expanded it into this published work. I want all my readers to benefit from it and enjoy reading it (Acts 4:12).

I must endeavor to point out that this is not a word-for-word, verse-and-chapter analysis or description or book of theology. It is better for the students and researchers to appreciate, understand, and enjoy Genesis and thus benefit from its exciting lessons rather than memorize everything. Therefore, humor is an essential part of this rather unique but truly enjoyable text. I have endeavored to include more than one viewpoint or school of thought pertaining to subjects of special interest, unique criteria, or pertinent scientific and historic value. My research is based upon expert opinions that I will quote as I expound on relevant data. Many of the opinions being offered are of a more sincere, conservative, and very positive approach because this, after all, is my legacy and my sincere Christian testimony. Also, I will use common language that the majority of my readers will find easy to understand, appreciate, and incorporate into their research. Students are not impressed by flamboyant vocabulary. I also believe that a more comprehensive bibliography can take the place of foot-notes. This well-documented work challenges students to do research on their own. Personal research is a vital component of the modern learning process. Truly hard and diligent work equals success! This book is of an apologetic or polemical nature, designed to expose the false teachings common to the conception of our origins and defend the obvious truth. Sadly, you and other students and teachers have been lied to so often by mass media and religious phonies. So finally, the truth must be told!

The student note pages located at the end of each chapter are lovingly provided for teachers, students, and researchers to record relevant data related to each chapter as well as new discoveries, current events, and test questions.

The scriptures I am quoting are taken from the King James Authorized Version of the Bible, which is an excellent literal translation of both the Ben Hayyim Massoretic text of the Old Testament and the Textus Receptus text of the New Testament. I truly believe this translation is one of the most literal translations we have available today, considering we no longer have the original autographs. Every version of the Holy Bible is a translation. I shall endeavor to provide a literal interpretation of Genesis and a fundamentalist viewpoint.

Remember that Genesis is a history book as well as Scripture and should be studied historically. There can possibly be too many difficulties with the neoorthodox, esoteric, and allegorical methods of interpretation, presenting the student with problems concerning history and related subjects such as science. The serious student should spend time in prayer before reading this book. Remember, most liberal professors are opposed to students gaining any exposure to the truth, especially when it is contrary to the false uniformitarian evolutionary agenda being taught today (Ezekiel 3). Good students must examine all points of view rather diligently and with an open mind and heart (Psalm 95), then analyze them carefully. May God, who created all things, guide you in your studies and bring you to all truth. May Genesis create in you an awareness of yourself in the diverse and rather complicated world around us. Truly, I personally, after much careful research, believe that it is wise to pray before reading this book and be prepared to be surprised!

The Bible is the holy Word of God. His Word is Truth (Jeremiah 29:13–14, 1 Peter 3:15). Early church Father St. Gerome stated that "ignorance of the scripture is ignorance of Christ." In reference to the Holy Bible, Queen Victoria said, "This Book is the secret of England's greatness." Abraham Lincoln stated, "I believe the Bible is the best gift God has given to man," and Theodore Roosevelt said that "no educated man can afford to be ignorant of the Bible." We have God's Word. Let's live by it.

It has never been against the law to teach the Bible or special creation in public schools in the United States. With the effects of secular humanism, paganism, eastern religions, Islam, antisemitism, multigenerism, pornography, neo-Darwinism, postmodernism, laziness, apathy, the occult, disrespect, and the new morality permeating every aspect of our modern society, political viewpoints are much more liberal. So this policy may soon change. The truth must be taught now while there is still time to do so (Ezekiel 33, John 3:16). So I strongly recommend that this book be used as a textbook or teacher's aide. Also, I grant permission for students and teachers to use this book in debates and discussions related to or concerning ancient history and origins; as a reference for term papers, tests, Bible studies, and classroom discussions; or endorsements usage. I may be contacted at the address below. I will answer all relevant and sincere correspondence sent to P.O. Box 1817, Brick, New Jersey 08724.

ACKNOWLEDGMENTS

I DESIRE TO honor all those servants of God listed below, whose encouragement and assistance aided me in the research as well as the editing and typing of this book. May God bless them always.

- Mimi MacMullen Koerner
- Richard Riss
- Bonnie Hill
- Diane-Lynn Broda
- Mary Kay Gunning Bonfante
- Richard Cannarella
- Anne B. Warren
- Irene P. Darmetko
- Somerset Christian College in Zarephath, New Jersey

A BRIEF ACADEMIC SURVEY

THE BOOK OF Genesis is the first book of the Torah (or Pentateuch) section of the Tanakh (or Old Testament), the Hebrew Scriptures. It is one of the five books of which authorship is traditionally attributed to Moses. As with all of Scripture, it is the Word of God in the words of man (2 Timothy 3:16, 2 Peter 1:21). Genesis was not the first book of the Bible to be recorded. The book of Job was written first. According to most available sources including the early church fathers and the ancient Rabbis, the book of Genesis was written approximately about 1400 BC—about six hundred to eight hundred years after Abraham was chosen by God. The wonderful Genesis account is the exciting introduction to God's plan for mankind. This is how the true and living God of the universe began to reveal Himself to us. The book of Genesis immediately introduced us to the concept of the Trinity, or God in three divine persons. Also, Genesis emphasizes that this planet, Earth, is exclusive in its purpose and nature. Life does not exist anywhere else.

The book of Genesis is foundational to understanding the rest of Scripture. Without the powerful and emotional accounts of creation, the fall of man, the results of sin, God's promised redemption, the deluge, and the Abrahamic covenant, the entire divinely inspired sixty-six books of the Bible would be mysterious and theologically incomprehensible. Truly, every other book in the Bible is based upon the vital information expounded upon in Genesis. Understanding our original origins as well as our past, present, and especially our future depends on Genesis. According to renowned author and Old Testament scholar Victor Hamilton, "few sections of the Old

Testament have been treated as thoroughly by scholars as has the Pentateuch." The truth is a strong foundation.

The title or name "Genesis" is the Greek word for "origin" or "beginning." Following Jewish tradition, the book was titled, or named, using its first Hebrew word, *bereshith*. In English, this is translated to "in the beginning." So the title provides us with some information explaining what the precious Holy Book is all about. When we read the Holy Bible, this is the perfect place to begin. Here we can start to unlock the mysteries of the entire Bible (Luke 18:21, John 8:32).

The word *Bible* is from the Greek word *biblos*, meaning "papyrus," a plant used for paper. According to Professors Hill and Walton, the writing of Genesis parallels ancient Mesopotamian literature. A very good example is the Sumerian or Shinarian Gilgamesh epic (read chapter 7). Many modern college professors all around the world share a common belief that the Genesis account, or divine epic, was partially derived from the Gilgamesh epic. This is because the information in both accounts of the deluge of Noah has many amazing similarities. I will present more detailed information on the deluge of Noah and explain how the Gilgamesh epic relates to the deluge presented in chapter 3 of this rather exciting history book.

Renowned Old Testament Professors Hill, Walten, Dillard, and Longman all agree that in the writing of Genesis, a toledoth formula was used in conjunction with a narrative literary genre. The *toledoth* of Adam, the *toledoth* of Cain and Abel, and the *toledoth* of Noah are fine examples. *Toledoth* means "family story." This method allows it to be easily understood, making Genesis one of the most popular books of the Bible. The word *generations* is used eleven times in Genesis, demonstrating that all of mankind is one family.

There are two exciting accounts of God's special creation in the book of Genesis. The first one (Genesis 1:1–31) presents us with a detailed order of events. The second creation account (Genesis 2:1–25) emphasizes the origin of mankind and wonderfully demonstrates God's sovereignty and love.

I must stress that the book of Genesis is not the opinions of man but divinely inspired. The Genesis account is God's own description of His special creation and our human origins. God created man in His own image and lovingly gave man dominion over all of nature (Genesis 1–2). Mankind has often abused that great privilege.

The book of Genesis contains some of the most exciting and revealing records of man's ancient history. For example, in Genesis, the important historical and religious significance of the Jewish patriarchs is recorded the testing of Abraham is a good example (see Chapter 6 of this Book). Their lives had a powerful effect upon man's early history. The meanings of the names of the patriarchs as well as other names recorded in Scripture are stories within themselves. In fact, they can be best described as a fascinating story within a story.

The book of Genesis is often referred to as two separate historical accounts. Genesis chapters 1 through 12 relate to mankind's origins and his ancient history. Chapters 12 through 50 deal mainly with the patriarchs of God's chosen people—the nation of Israel—and the ancient world around them. In fact, the next 905 chapters after Genesis in the Tanakh, or Old Testament, are a wonderful historical record of the descendants of Abraham and the lineage of the promised Messiah, the Lord Jesus.

The book of Genesis expressed itself with theology rather than philosophy. Truly, Genesis is the basis for most of our Judeo-Christian theology. No other history book has had the powerful impact of Genesis. This is due mainly to its inspired content and cultural context. Denial of any portion of this book negates all of Holy Scripture. To believe, it must be all or nothing at all (Revelation 3:15–16, Hebrews 11:3). We have the truth!

The book of Genesis is one of the most accurate records of man's spiritual history available. Dr. H. Morris of the Institute for Creation Research (or ICR) in California, USA, teaches that Genesis does not talk about an agelong struggle upward from chaos. Rather, it tells us of an originally perfect creation of a beautifully designed, perfectly ordered cosmos marred later by man's sin. So the book of Genesis teaches us about the fall of man and the tragic results of sin. It also talks about God's love and mercy toward mankind after the fall. Because of the new morality, this biblical world viewpoint is usually no longer taught in public schools. Sadly, so much of our history has been either rewritten or deliberately hidden from twenty-first-century students. Our past history is often classified with rather impressive titles such as the Stone Age or Iron Age. Unfortunately for the students, these titles have a tendency to award undue credible support to the popular uniformitarian evolutionary worldview. However, God's Word is always true, so put your faith in it and believe.

Genesis introduces us to the evil, frightening concept of sin. The important but ominous theme of the eternal struggle that stated when mankind sinned by disobeying our righteous God was the beginning of everything evil or horrible. It is the effects of sin that produced man's guilt, fear, sickness, poverty, pain, suffering, sorrow, and death. Sin is the cause of every trouble. In fact, the terrible results of sin, which are mentioned for the first time in history after the fall of man in Genesis 5:6, is repeated over and over again throughout our bloody human history, proving that all of mankind needs redemption through God's promised Messiah. Shamefully, the convoluted, unscientific, and erroneous belief in evolution is the evident result of man's sin. We can never avoid our true carnal nature. Only God can help us avoid punishment for sin through His holy Messiah. Therefore, the book of Genesis displays God's love. Prophecies describing the promised Messiah, the Lord Jesus, are first mentioned in Genesis. His pre-existence (Genesis 1:26), His being born of a woman (Genesis 1:15) and the seed of Abraham (Genesis 12:3), and His being from the tribe of Judah (Genesis 49:10) begin His Messianic résumé. Although almost the entire Bible speaks and prophecies of Him, without the Genesis account, we would not completely understand His Messianic purpose and love.

Students usually want to know when Genesis took place or fit into history. But remember, historians are often prejudiced, misinformed, controversial people. So also remember that if I quote the evil opinions of Hitler, that does not make me a Nazi or prove that I agree with his twisted, sinful, dangerous teachings. Comparative research has its opinions and advantages. Archbishop Usher dates Genesis as taking place between 4004 BC and 1805 BC. However, Canadian missionary David Brewer from the Life in Messiah ministry states that Dr. Usher did not realize that there are significant gaps in the genealogies of Genesis 5 and Genesis 10. when they are compared to 1 Corinthians 1:9, Matthew 1, and Luke 3:23–28, according to Professor R. Riss, the Genesis account took place from antiquity to about 1805 BC (Richard Riss is the professor and assistant dean of Church History at Pillar Christian College in New Jersey and my mentor). Professor Collins of the Institute of Biblical and Theological Studies in New Mexico, USA, believes that Genesis occurred from antiquity to 1805 BC or 1806 BC. Remember that when I quote someone, I am not always supporting their views. So according to H. Camping, of radio fame (or sometimes "shame"), Genesis took place from 11013 BC to about 1806 BC. Prof. Riss may agree with Rev. Dr. Usher. Mr. Camping strongly disagrees with Rev. Dr. Usher. I do NOT support Mr. Camping's teachings or theology, but that's predictable. However, I will use his time line as a comparative example when used along with astute and well-recognized scholarship. Many Christians including myself consider him a false prophet. However, most time lines available to students today may have major differences in dating the time of Genesis, so diligent students will research and compare the available data from all relevant sources. The evidence suggests that only when the phrase "called His name" is used is there a reference to an immediate descendant. Students must be aware of the long Biblical time lines or chronologic genealogy lists that do not always represent immediate descendants or family trees. Rather, they can represent relevant points in time in the history of the Jewish people. Truly, all of mankind's history, either directly or indirectly, revolves around God's chosen Jewish people and the descendants of Shem. I will discuss this in more detail in my chapter on the Table of Nations.

Our moral and ethical character is affected by how we view the book of Genesis and the Holy Bible. The renowned Bible commentator Derek Kidner wrote that "there can scarcely be another part of Scripture over which so many battles, theological, scientific, historical, and literary have been fought, or so many strong opinions cherished." It is vitally important to study Genesis. Our future outlook on life depends on it. The amazing book of Genesis clearly demonstrates God's holy, righteous standards and mankind's obligation to obey, appreciate, and live according to them. Remember that our loving, holy, and always-forgiving God knows what's best for us. However, students should also consider that our knowledge of absolute truth, our sin, our sinful nature, our environment, peer pressure, and our origins affect human behavior.

It is very important to have an understanding and knowledge of Ancient Near Eastern history and culture to best understand the book of Genesis. In the Near East, the land of ancient Canaan, which is now known as modern-day Israel, is the primary place that God chose to reveal Himself to the world (all of mankind). The exciting history of God's chosen Jewish people took place there. Also, the Messiah, the Lord Jesus, lived, taught, died, and arose from the dead there. That's why it is called the Holy Land. The evidence is available to modern man. Just read the Bible. Archaeology has provided us with much information (refer to the last chapter). God worked out His plan for our salvation in conjunction with the culture at that time and place in history. I would love it if God had chosen the British Isles, but God chose Israel. Students may try to understand Genesis in the context of our own modern, fast-paced, technical culture. This is a mistake. We are living in a very different society today from that in the world of Genesis. Twenty-first century values are rather situational and complicated. However, the sinful nature of man and the forgiving love of God have not changed since man's fall. God is good all the time. To understand Genesis, we must first understand God's love and also our weak human nature. Our propensity to sin always controls our actions.

In reference to our weak, sinful human nature, it is very important to realize that after our original ancestors Adam and Eve sinned and disobeyed God, our human nature drastically changed. Mankind became mortal, evil, and very rebellious. So God gave us His handbook, the Bible. Truly, Genesis is so important to us all, who are sinners, that it can—if used sincerely and properly—become God's handbook for man's repentant lifestyle. It's because of our sinful nature that we need the "Christ or Messiah. But God loves us regardless of our circumstances (1 Peter 4:1 & 2).

The Lord Jesus also quoted Genesis. This alone makes the book of Genesis valid. His divine, authoritative references to Genesis are as follows: Matthew 19:4–6, 24:37–39; Mark 10:4–9; Luke 11:49–51, 17:26–32; and John 7:44. Denial of the validity of Genesis is calling Christ a liar (John 14:6). According to the well-known British history authors Eisenman and Wise, the Dead Sea Scrolls contain excerpts from the Holy Bible identical to our Scripture today (KJV). We have the truth! Truly, Genesis is God's Holy Word given to us to teach us about our origins, His plan for us, and our future hope in Christ (John 8:32).

GENESIS OUTLINE

1. Creation account (Genesis 1:1–2:25)
2. The fall of man and sin (Genesis 3:1–24)
3. The *toledoth* of Cain and Abel (Genesis 4:1–18)
4. The deluge, or *toledoth*, of Noah (Genesis 6–9)
5. The Tower of Babel (Genesis 11:1–9)
6. The Table of Nations (Genesis 11:10–Genesis 32)
7. The *toledoths* of Abraham and Isaac (Genesis 12–25:19)
8. The *toledoth* of Jacob (Genesis 25:20–36:43)
9. The *toledoth* of Joseph (Genesis 37–50)
10. Proverbs 3:5

CREATION/ORIGINS

CHAPTER 1

Creation/Origins

EVERYTHING HAS A reason and a purpose for being. God created everything (ex nihilo) from nothing. He spoke, and all things came into being (Genesis 1, Psalm 33:6–9). Before creation, God already had considered man's fall and planned for our redemption (Revelation 13:8). God's plan is the theme, the underlying idea, expressed through the entire sixty-six books of the Bible, starting with Genesis. God's wonderful creation of the earth and the entire universe works to demonstrate His love, power, mercy, and glory to man. God provided us with a perfect environment to live in. The planet Earth is exclusive, and everything in it is especially designed for man. Life does not exist anywhere else (Psalm 115:15–16, 1 Corinthians 15).

The Holy Bible, or Tanakh, begins with the simple statement "In the beginning, God created Heaven and the Earth" (Genesis 1:1). Truly, the Book of Genesis does not try to prove the existence of God because the evidence of His beautiful creation speaks for Him (Romans 1:20). What we are able to see or perceive is but a tiny speck of the infinite universe around us, displaying His glory (Psalm 8:3–4). All of nature has design and purpose, engineered by the Master Craftsman, our loving God. There are many fascinating creation stories around the world. The ancient Babylonian record depicts creation as the result of the sexual union of the mythological gods Apsu and Tiamat. In the Ancient Egyptian creation story, the sky goddess Nut and the earth god Geb gave form to the world. The biblical and pagan accounts are very different in origin. Only God's Word reveals the truth (Isaiah 45:5, Romans 3:4).

Creation was accomplished by God in a literal six-day period. On the Sabbath, or seventh day, God rested from all His works (Genesis 2:2). The book of Genesis describes each day of creation in detail. Every important aspect of God's special creation is recorded in proper order of occurrence. With respect to chapter 1, verses 4 and 14, there is a controversy as to how light or day and night could have existed before the creation of the Sun in Genesis 1:16–18. But when the student is serious about the truth, takes the entire Bible into consideration, and compares the Genesis record with Revelation 21:23, it is quite convincing that light did exist before the sun. (The Lord was the light.) This fact makes the book of Genesis easy to accept and believe. All of Holy Scripture is related to the vital information in Genesis. Many modern scientists claim that life originated in the oceans. However, Genesis 1:12 teaches us that life was first created on land two days before it was created in the oceans. You may have been taught that the warm-blooded birds evolved from cold-blooded reptiles or dinosaurs. But there is no tangible evidence found anywhere on Earth to support this hypothesis. These creatures have completely different metabolisms; therefore, one could never have given rise to the other. However, in the Genesis account, we read that birds were created before reptiles (Genesis 1:20–25). According to God's plan, the earth was created first. The Sun, Moon, stars, and universe were made later to show God's glory and power. Scripture clearly shows us that life in the oceans was not created until after the universe was created. When we examine the known universe around us, we can only begin to understand God and creation. It would take scientists an eternity to begin to comprehend everything that's out there. Man's knowledge is very limited (Isaiah 55:8). In 2 Peter 8, it says that according to God, "one day is as a thousand years old." Also, see Psalm 90:9. This sometimes can be misinterpreted or taken out of context to mean that Earth's day of creation was a thousand years or more. But even some evolutionists can tell that is wrong.

Evolutionists teach us that Earth is approximately 4.5 or 4.67 billion years old. To my knowledge, this is based upon the false geological column and upon the carbon-14 and potassium-argon methods of dating. These methods of dating, however, have been proven to be ineffective. An article in *Science*, vol. 141 (1963), stated that a living mollusk was tested by carbon 14. The readings showed that it had been dead for three thousand years. In the *Journal of Geophysical Research*, volume 3 (1968), we read that when lava rocks were tested in Hawaii by the potassium-argon method, they measured an age of almost 3 billion years; but the lava had been produced by the volcano in 1801. These methods of scientific dating should always work in situations where scientists know the age of the subject being tested. But obviously, they do not work at all! The modern radiometric dating techniques are in serious error. The false geologic column is based solely upon index fossils located in stratum, with impressive scientific-sounding names such as Jurassic, Cambrian, or Mesozoic Ages. It was invented or founded upon the false assumption that evolution is a proven fact. It is important for the student to realize that nowhere in the world does the geologic column actually occur. So the entire concept is false! It only exists in the imagination of the evolutionist. Sadly, Darwin's busy evolutionists will waste time and money monkeying around and are afraid to tell the truth.

We live on a young Earth. In fact, the process of erosion proves that Earth is very young. According to geology expert Dr. John Morris, the sediment flowing into the oceans is 27.5 billion tons per year. So it would take 14 million years for all of our continents to completely erode into the sea. If Earth were 1 billion years old, our continents would have eroded away some seventy times! So Earth is not 4.5 or 4.67 billion years old. Basing their research upon recorded history, true science, and God's Holy Word, the majority of Bible scholars believe Genesis places the age of Earth and the universe at about six to seven thousand years old. We cannot yet be sure of an exact date. Science and archaeology as well as history support Genesis (refer to chapter 7 and *Primal Man* by Chick).

Unlike the animals, man was created in the image of God. See Psalm 8. Also, he was humbly formed from the dust of the earth. In Genesis 1:26, God said, "Let us make man in our image, after our likeness." The words *us* and *our* in this passage refer to the Trinity. The Trinity, or Elohim, is God the Father, God the Son, and God the Holy Spirit. Christians believe that God is a plurality in unity or has a triune nature. Please see Isaiah 48:12–16, Psalm 2:7–12, and John 14. Man is also a triunity consisting of a body, a spirit, and a soul. The early church councils of Nicaea (AD 325) and Constantinople (AD 381) established the Trinity as a cornerstone of Christian theology. The Trinity is defined as one Holy God in three divine persons.

In Genesis 2:8, we read about the garden of Eden, or paradise—a place where everything was exceptionally beautiful and perfect. The garden was designed by God as a place to test man. In Eden, God gave mankind (Adam and Eve) only one rule to obey: they were not to eat the forbidden fruit of the tree of knowledge. But they failed the test and lost paradise. Scholars have debated the exact location of the garden of Eden for centuries. The location is traditionally believed to be between the Tigris and Euphrates Rivers, in what is now known as Iraq (Genesis 2:10–14). Many teachers may believe that the Persian Gulf now covers the area where Eden was located. A growing number of scholars including biblical antiquities expert Dr. Role believe the garden of Eden was located around the area of present-day Northern Iraq where all the rivers in Genesis 2:10–14 have their beginning or source, or headwaters. Michael Saunders of the Bible Research Foundation in California believes the garden of Eden is in Eastern Turkey. In this region, Saunders identified four rivers and linked them to the four rivers described in Genesis. During Roman times, the Jewish historian Josephus believed that Eden included the entire fertile crescent, from India to Egypt. However, because of the mass destruction caused by the deluge of Noah and thousands of years of erosion, it is difficult to find the exact location. According to Bible history authors Professor R. Riss and H. H. Halley, the ancient city of Eridu was constructed on the sight of the Garden of Eden after the Deluge, or Flood. The amazing ruins of Eridu (Abu Shahrain) are located approximately twelve miles south of ancient Ur.

In Genesis 2:18, we read that God stated, "It is not good for man to be alone." This statement strongly suggests that Adam, who was created to have a personal relationship with God, was lonely. It was said that Adam was complete, yet he was also incomplete. He desired to have more of his own kind, a suitable mate. So God created Eve from Adam's rib while he was sleeping. It was God who created marriage and the family (Genesis 2:23–25). The family unit is a gift from God. The family is man's social and economic unit, designed by God for our benefit and health. Divorce was not part of God's plan but is one of the results of man's deadly sin (Matthew 5:32). The Bible defines marriage as a sacred, holy union or bond between one man and one woman. Sincere students should carefully read Leviticus, Deuteronomy, and Jude. Any other form of marriage is a sin (Ephesians 5:28–29). God only created two genders, only male and female. Remember, God said so. The modern transgender trends are wrong.

In chapter 3 of Genesis, we read that according to His plan, God tested man's obedience. Satan, in the form of a snake or serpent, was allowed by God to test Eve and, through her, Adam as well. She and Adam disobeyed God by eating the forbidden fruit, causing all mankind to sin (the original sin). We do not know what kind of fruit it was. The emphasis here is on sin, not the fruit. I know that when most people today are confronted by God's holiness, sin becomes an extremely uncomfortable subject. But most of man's history is a direct result of sin, so it cannot be avoided or ignored (Psalm 51:3–4). There was no death until mankind committed sin. Creation was made perfect, but sin entered the world. Death, both physical and spiritual, came into the world as the negative result of man's sin (Genesis 3:3, Romans 5:12, 6:23). Sin is a willful or intentional disobedience against the perfect will of our holy God. Adam and Eve experienced deep feelings of guilt and shame and had to make clothes out of fig leaves to cover their nakedness and sin (Genesis 2:25). Adam and Eve did not accept the personal responsibilities for their actions (sin). Adam blamed both God and Eve. Eve blamed the serpent, or devil. God is holy and righteous and cannot allow sin in His presence. Sin destroyed mankind's intimate relationship with God and changed human nature. Man's original state of innocence was lost. This is known as the fall of man. Man's sin had a devastating negative effect on all of nature, the Hebrew Calendar overlaps ours, but traditionally rabbinical teaching dates the creation of humanity in September. So, some teachers can place the fall of man in October possibly on the 31st. But this has not been proven. Sadly, nothing in

God's creation has ever been the same since Adam and Eve rebelled against God and committed the deadly original sin. Mankind now needed to be redeemed and reconciled to God. Adam and Eve were evicted from Eden and forbidden by God to return. Fellowship with God had to be restored (Isaiah 59:1–2, Acts 3:18–21). According to most Christian and Jewish theologians, in Genesis 3:14–15, God promised mankind a Redeemer or Messiah who would bruise the head of the serpent, or devil, restoring the relationship. There are two comings of the Messiah—first as God's suffering servant (Psalm: 22) and second as the ruling King (Jer.:23).

The famous Messianic Jewish scholar Dr. Ferchtenbaum of Dallas Theological Seminary and renowned clergyman Messianic Rabbi M. Baleston of Beth Messiah in New Jersey believe that Genesis 4:1 teaches us that Eve believed that when Cain was born, he was the promised Messiah. They teach that modern English versions of the Bible translate that passage as "Gotten a man from the Lord"; but in the original Hebrew, Eve states, "I have gotten a man child, the Lord." Knowledge of Hebrew is important for proper exegesis. The ancient Jewish tradition states that Eve had twenty-three sons and twenty-three daughters, which includes Cain's, Abel's, and Seth's wives.

Getting back to the subject of sin as the cause of death, there is much to consider. Because of our carnal, sinful nature, it is impossible for mankind to live holy lives unless we rely on God's mercy and grace through the Messiah, Lord Jesus. Most modern-day, twenty-first-century scientists and historians do not believe in sin or the results of sin, so they cannot accept the book of Genesis as a true historical record. They believe that sin is an outmoded religious concept used to discipline children. Yet it is evident that the obvious actions of mankind demonstrate that everything we do is in some way affected by sin. Their opinion about sin is the result of sin. Also, the biblical fact that no one died until man sinned is considered to be mythological by evolutionists. They believe death was always present and preceded the religious concept of sin. But students must consider this serious controversy very carefully. If death is a natural process of evolution and not as a result of sin, then the atoning death of the promised Savior, the Lord Jesus, was unnecessary (Isaiah 53). The blood atonement for sin is part of the plan of God and is found throughout Scripture, proving the Genesis account to be reliable and true (Leviticus 17:11; Exodus 12; Romans 3:23, 14:12). So please carefully research this important topic. Science and medicine, and religion cannot cure sin. Truly, the Lord Jesus is the promised Messiah (Isaiah 53, John 14:6). Over three hundred fulfilled Old Testament prophecies confirm this truth.

Scientists and historians have tried to prove or disprove the existence of Adam and Eve (Genesis 1–2). One of the best proofs of their existence is the fact that every nation on Earth and every culture of mankind worships deity. Man has a natural awareness, or inner concept, of God. No animal has this ability. The Creation Research Institute in California, USA, teaches us that recent genetic research has proven that all people living today can trace their lineage back to one original woman. Also, the author and geneticist Spencer Wells has discovered that both genetics and the Bible show us that there is a common origin of all humanity. All people living today descended from Adam and Eve. Now you may ask, "Why do evolutionists refuse to accept the evidence and refuse to recognize God and creation?" This is because a sinful heart interprets science and nature incorrectly. Regenerated Christians understand truth and beauty through God's Holy Spirit, which is present in every believer (2 Corinthians 2:14, Deuteronomy 29:9, Romans 1). Understanding and accepting this truth makes people more accountable to God. Evolutionists do not desire this awesome responsibility.

In Genesis 4, we read the *toledoth*, or family story, of Cain and Abel. This is a good example of blood atonement through sacrificial offering. Abel's offering was acceptable to God because a lamb was offered and Abel offered his very best. The lamb is prophetic and symbolic throughout Scripture, pertaining to the sacrifice of the Messiah, Lord Jesus, as God's Lamb, atoning for our sins (John 1:29, Revelation 5:6, Exodus 12). When Cain offered vegetables, it was not symbolic of God's Messiah. Cain did it his way, not God's way. This is how religion is created. Religion is man's effort to reconcile himself to God. All religions go against God's perfect plan. The biblically based relationship achieved through Christ's blood atonement is God's perfect plan. The Lord Jesus suffered, died, and then rose from the dead to pay the penalty or punishment for the sins of mankind. So just like Abel's sacrifice, God gave us His very best. Everything God gives us is His best. The Lord Jesus is God in human form as the incarnation.

We will return to Cain and Abel; however, first, let's examine some rather powerful and amazing but seldom-taught proven scientific facts regarding nature, intelligent design, truth, and special creation. Darwin was wrong (John 8:32–36). According to Dr. D. Gish of the Institute for Creation Research, Earth was created perfectly to support life. Earth's diameter is eight thousand miles. If Earth were just a little larger or a little smaller, life as we know it would be impossible. The Earth is tilted at twenty-three and a half degrees to the perpendicular. It was perfectly placed there to create the four seasons we enjoy and allow more land to support crops to feed us. The Earth could NEVER have evolved in this way or been formed by chance. Science author Thomas Heinz teaches us that the rocks and soil on Earth prove that Earth is truly very young. He states that "if rocks formed over billions of years, the steady rain of meteors would show up in great quantities in the soil." However, Earth's meteor count shows us that Earth is only thousands of years old, not billions of years old. Also, the absence of a thick layer of cosmic dust upon the moon speaks clearly of a young solar system and universe.

Science education specialist Fred Wilson from ICR (the Institute for Creation Research in California) teaches us that in God's creation, there exists a "divine proportion" that is exhibited in a multitude of shapes, numbers, and patterns whose relationship can only be the result of the omnipotent, good, and all-wise God of Scripture. This divine proportion—existing in the smallest to the largest parts in living and also in nonliving things—reveals the awesome handiwork of God and His interest in beauty, function, and order. So God's fingerprints are on all of creation.

A theory always requires observation and testing the hypothesis of evolution always teaches us that the greater amount of genetic material that a creature or living organism has, then the more advanced it becomes. But true science has proven otherwise! One amazing scientific fun fact truly demonstrates that frogs have much more genetic DNA material than humans. Yet humans are far more advanced than frogs, proving that evolution is a lie and not a theory and not at all scientific. So unsurprisingly, special creation is the truth. The answers are found in the Bible, in the book of Genesis. When referring to special creation, British scientist and TV celebrity Dr. Stephen Hawking stated, "It would be very difficult to explain why the universe should have begun in just this way except, as the act of God intended it to create beings like us."

There are more than an ample number of books available that demonstrate scientific evidence that supports special creation. I recommend that the diligent student read *Scientific Creationism* by Morris and *The Collapse of Evolutionism* by Huse. These books support the book of Genesis in its entirety and provide detailed information that I will not supply in this rather brief but informative history book (Colossians 1:16).

Now let's return to Cain and Abel and continue to explore Genesis. In Genesis 4:8–15, we read about the first murder. Abel pleased God and had favor with God. Cain did not. Many theologians believe that it was out of envy that Cain killed his brother Abel, for he had inherited the ability to sin from Adam and Eve. Remember that after the fall of man, as part of God's judgment, Adam and Eve had a sinful or carnal nature that was transferred to all generations starting with Cain and Abel. Cain's question "Am I my brother's keeper?" is a statement of callous indifference that is expressed often throughout our violent human history. However, we indeed are our brother's keeper, so many Christian missions and charities have been established throughout the world. After Abel was murdered by his brother Cain, a third son, Seth, was born to Adam and Eve. All of humanity now living today can trace their lineage back to Seth (Romans 5:12, Deuteronomy 30:19).

The mark of Cain is an interesting subject and an excellent example of God's grace. To protect Cain from having to receive vengeance because of his sin, our merciful God placed a mark upon Cain (Genesis 4:14–15). This is similar to Revelation 13. I was told to be aware that in the modern world today, every barcode has three sixes. We do not know what the mark of Cain looked like. Perhaps it was a brand, birthmark, or tattoo. As to its form, the mark of Cain might have looked like a tree, symbolic of the original tree in the garden of Eden that contained the forbidden fruit. Still, others may believe the mark of Cain was some kind of light so he could be spotted from a distance or horns like a bull. I think it might have been a cross or lamb, symbolic of God's redemption plan (Exodus 12), or perhaps it was three sixes, the mark of the Beast (Revelation 13) or a QR code. We don't know what it looked like, but we do know it worked. It is generally believed that Cain lived safely for hundreds of years (Genesis 4:17). The longevity of people living before the deluge will be discussed in another chapter. All things work for our good and according to God's purpose (see Romans 8). God decides how long we live (Job 12:10, Psalm 90).

By now, some of you students are saying that I have a creationist presupposition. You may still believe in evolution and the awesome big bang theory. However, true science based upon facts, not religious beliefs, proves to us that special creation is the only logical, viable choice. Now let's examine the truth.

The first law of thermodynamics states that matter and energy can be converted from one form to another but only converted, not created or destroyed. Therefore, the universe did not create itself or evolve into its present state. So there was no big bang. Also, the entire universe is expanding outward in all directions without a defined center or ends. Its speed is constantly accelerating at an alarming rate. If the big bang had occurred, then the universe would've had a well-defined center and not be accelerating at all. It would be rapidly slowing down (Jeremiah 31:31). Also, any big bang or explosion always causes chaos and never produces order. The known universe is extremely orderly! The sobering facts speak for themselves. Evolution is a big lie destroying lives but making big profits in the process, and it is not based on science! So evolution is one of the most evil ideas ever conceived by the heart of man.

The second law of thermodynamics governs the process of the conservation of energy, which is known as entropy. This law states that everything in the known universe is going from a complicated to a simple state of being. Left to themselves, all things decay. For evolution to take place, the exact opposite must occur: this law must work in reverse. Evolution is therefore impossible. The book of Genesis gives us the true account. Scientific facts do not lie. After you consider science and its facts, you will need MUCH more faith to believe in evolution (Hebrews 11–3). So evolution is religious but not scientific (Psalm 104:2)!

Today, in the dawn of the twenty-first century, the majority of the secular college professors question the real existence of absolute truth. They teach that there is no longer a concept of right and wrong or good and evil but that without any absolutes, there is complete chaos. So in our enlightened new age of no absolutes except vodka, it is very difficult to know the truth. But many students are researching on their own and discovering that special creation and the book of Genesis are still the absolute truth. So the only logical action is to act upon this truth. Freedom from the negative results of sin can only be achieved through faith in the Lord Jesus! Salvation is a matter of repentant trust and obedience with sincerity, so share your heart with Him and discover that He is absolutely the Messiah, God, and the Creator. (Jer. 29:31), (Peter 5:5) and (John 3:11). Author Chris Francis stated that 'the crucification was the payment for sin. The Resurrection is the receipt (John 3:16) and (John 11:25-26).

The loveliness of creation is an expression of God's love for us. So please consider the vital fact that mankind is gifted above all of God's earthly creatures, with the rather unique ability to truly appreciate, understand, and enjoy the natural beauty that God has created (Matthew 28:6, John 14:11). The wonderful works of our loving God can be cherished by those individuals who take the time to experience them. Remember, the glory of God is everywhere, waiting to be discovered and explored (Job 39, Psalm 95).

When he was reflecting upon the beauty of nature, poet John Lubbock wrote, "Earth and sky, woods and fields, lakes and rivers, the mountains and the sea, are excellent schoolmasters, and teach some of us more than we can ever learn from books." Nature always gives testimony to God's glory and to God's love. Poet Orson Sweet

Marden's description of nature is also worth our heart's attention: "Forest, lakes and rivers, clouds and winds, stars and flowers, stupendous glaciers, and crystal snowflakes—every form of animate or inanimate existence, leaves its impression upon the soul of man." Nature always energizes the soul. Enjoy God's creation.

Creation all around us must be considered very carefully for us to fully appreciate the love of God. In the fast-paced, rather technical twenty-first century, we are living in a very crowded and extremely stressful society plagued with far too many serious problems. For many of us, life can be a painful existence. I myself have often experienced anxiety and suffering as a result of our youth-centered, secularized, narcissistic society. Most of us are living far from the handiwork of our loving and forgiving God. Our sprawling urban environments are vivid and powerful expressions of man's technical achievements. Just like the Tower of Babel (chapter 4), this is not God's glory! Remember that sin is everywhere and that mankind glorifies himself. It is evident that too many of us do not take the time to fully appreciate and really enjoy the marvelous creation of which we human beings were granted dominion and responsibility over and are a wonderful part. The book of Genesis can help us begin that privileged process. Remember, we were created on purpose with purpose. One of the best ways to really enjoy and understand God's love is to spend time experiencing the beauty and wonder of God's natural world. We must stop destroying our environment. Everywhere we go, the environment used to reflect the glory of God, but there are always places filled with serenity, beauty, and God's natural peace and purpose. If we love God, we should preserve what's left of His precious nature. So let's give God the glory with our hopes and accomplishments and commune with nature today (Psalm 104, 89:12).

STUDENT'S NOTES

PRIMITIVE OR ADVANCED

CHAPTER 2

Primitive or Advanced

ONE OF THE most important issues to be dealt with in the search for our origins is this awesome question: "Was early man a primitive, cave-dwelling savage, or was early man quite civilized?" The answer to this question is relevant not only to our understanding of man's origins and antiquities but will also shed light on the unsolved mysteries of man's early history. Our moral and ethical behavior is based upon how we as individuals answer this question (John 8:32). This is why the student must explore all possibilities before forming an opinion. The secular history books concerning origins, for the most part, do not have any real evidence to support their amazing and sensational but widely believed and accepted claims, so they often rely upon the false neo-Darwinism rather than true science. But the book of Genesis has more than enough archaeological, scientific, and historical evidence to prove its validity (Romans 3–4). Please refer to the evidence presented in chapters 1 and 7 of this exciting textbook.

Teachers and scholars may need to know that some of the rather serious information I am about to powerfully but lovingly present in this awakening, shocking, and very controversial chapter, including many new surprises and historical evidence, may create a negative response from students who are closed-minded and reject ancient artifacts and truth concerning ancient history and our ancestors. This is why modern man often rewrites history. So I sincerely advise that my readers have an open mind and approach this new knowledge with a purely academic attitude. However, most students will be well-informed, surprised, rather intrigued, and quite amazed by the new information presented and carefully examined in this unique chapter.

Today, in many modern Bible colleges, professors and theologians now realize that the origins of mankind can foster many differences of opinion among students and teachers regarding whether or not ancient man was primitive or advanced. It is a question that must be answered correctly. I will now answer this important, controversial question by presenting both views as they are taught today.

We will first examine the popular neo-Darwinist evolutionary viewpoint. According to Dr. Spielvogel of Pennsylvania State University, as quoted from his famous book about Western civilization, mankind originated from primates that evolved into hominids. Then man slowly improved upward over millions of years, thus becoming *Homo sapiens*. Dr. Spielvogel teaches that the original *Homo sapiens* were Paleolithic hunters and gatherers. Then man advanced to a Neolithic farming stage. Eventually, man became the civilized urban creature that we are today. This is the common belief among the majority of the liberal teachers, scientists, and historians and is considered to be a cornerstone of both our popular and academic culture (Psalm 119:128). If this is true, then hominids should still exist today, so where are they?

So as you just read, according to Dr. Spielvogel's informative, uniformitarian, and rather fascinating teaching on the subject of evolution, scholars can logically assume that a nomadic hunter-gather and farmer or agriculturists are still primitive. We can assume that because of these occupations, they are of a lower stage of human development. But they themselves and most modern scientists strongly disagree with this erroneous, uniformitarian hypothesis even if evolutionists use Dr. Spielvogel's logic to support evolution; and they often do so. In fact, ignoring Dr. Speilvogel's logic, the majority of scholars today believe everyone living in the twenty-first century—regardless of their present race, location, lifestyle or occupation—is advanced. However, the constant upgrading or improvement to advanced technology does not always prove that man is advanced even if their present technology appears to be primitive or obsolete and even if evolution is based upon this teaching. So I believe that our technology always represents or acts as an extension of our lifestyles, our environment, our education, and ourselves.

Yet according to the readily available, truly scientific, and historical data and the information in chapter 1 of this book, Earth is too young for the hypothesis of evolution to occur. Earth and universe are quite possible only six to seven thousand years old, not the millions of years required by uniformitarian evolution. According to the popular author and scientist Thomas Heinze, the incredible design and amazing complexity of a single living cell truly demands an intelligent designer. And renowned Dr. Crick, the world-famous genetics pioneer and expert, stated that "human DNA could not have evolved by chance." So the experts repudiate or reject evolution in favor of special creation. Also, according to Dr. Huse, evolution is mathematically impossible; and Professor Frederick Hoyle of Cambridge University stated that "the likelihood of the formation of life from inanimate matter is one out of 1,040,000." Dr. Huse can add hundreds of zeros to that rather large number. Obviously but not surprisingly, there is no real tangible evidence to support evolution, just a lot of guessing and pretending such as "may have been," "hardly changed," "was possible then," "might have happened," "probably existed," "could have been," etc. It sounds like a lot of monkey business to me.

The book of Genesis vividly demonstrates that mankind was an advanced and civilized being from the beginning of creation. Immediately mankind began exhibiting amazing, highly developed skills in the fields of science, art, culture, religion, music, and technology. There are some theologians, such as John Wesley, who believed that after the fall of man, sin diminished the mental abilities of humans and animals. This is to some degree quite evident. Down syndrome, fragile X syndrome, cerebral palsy, arthritis, and muscular dystrophy are some sobering examples of our human deterioration. The most obvious example of animal deterioration is the loss of speech (Genesis 3:1–5). Although sin has had a sad and devastating effect on human nature for over six thousand years, our advanced skills have remained intact. Even though we have diminished mental abilities, our scientific and technical achievements throughout history are impressive, demonstrating that we were created by a loving God.

In Genesis 1:26, we read that God made man in His own image and likeness. No other earthly creature has been more endowed with the godlike capabilities as has man. The famous antiquities expert and world traveler Dr. Chittick from George Fox College, in his ongoing research, teaches that early man was highly capable and intelligent, accomplishing wonderful things that seem impossible by today's standards. So human nature was always advanced. Mankind is uniquely created by God, and has a special purpose. To be human is a privilege, not an excuse.

Cain and Abel exhibited highly advanced skills right from the beginning. In Genesis 4:2–5, we read that Abel was a keeper of sheep but that Cain was a tiller of the ground. Abel had to have skills in domesticating animals and animal husbandry. Cain displayed skills in organized agriculture. These are significant accomplishments. Genesis 4:17 informs us that Cain built a city for his son. Please consider that man had already advanced this far in only two generations of development. This is not an example of cave-dwelling primitive savages (Romans 1:22).

Early man's highly developed skills in music and sophisticated skills in the art of metallurgy are mentioned in Genesis 4:20–22. First, we read that Jubal was the father of those who handle the harp and organ. These musical instruments are not primitive but advanced, and they are difficult to play unless one is gifted by God with the talent that is necessary to do so. We also read that Tubal-Cain was a forger or an instructor of every artifice in brass and iron. So early man possessed the highly crafted arts of smelting and refining metals. These skills were in practice long before the supposed or pretended Stone Age, Bronze Age, or Iron Age, which are so widely accepted by teachers and students today. Period/age titles can present the student with a false uniformitarian view of man's early history. Our best resource for the truth is God's Holy Word, the Bible. According to Dr. Chittick of George Fox College, "it is an error to assume that (early) man was not mentally capable, or that he was ignorant of what we call science, and scientific principle." The ancients knew we were created and never evolved! I believe that much of the truth has yet to be discovered and discerned.

Man is creative and innovative in a way that no other earthly creature can match because he was designed that way. Only man records history. Only man understands mathematics, chemistry, and physics. Bees build hives, spiders weave elaborate webs, ants construct colonies, and beavers build canals and dams; but no animal can ever approach man's abilities, creativity, wisdom, variety, and originality. Animals build their homes according to a fixed program (instinct). This remarkable evidence suggests the program originated with the divine, loving Creator, not with the creature. Mankind was specially created with exceptional highly advanced skills right from the beginning, in the image of God (see Genesis 1:27). Intelligence is a God-ordained privilege.

Much of our prehistory remains a mystery; however, many discoveries are constantly being made that not only support the book of Genesis but also the fact that early or ancient man was not a primitive savage but was quite advanced. One of the major proofs is OOPArts. OOPArts are out-of-place artifacts often discovered in archaeological digs or tells, ancient tombs, and caves. These objects are often considered too advanced to have been discovered where they were found (e.g., there are rumors or reports of toys resembling model airplanes being found in Ancient Egyptian tombs). I will provide more examples. So once again, prepare to be delightfully surprised. Modern Darwinian evolutionary thought teaches us that artifacts should be increasingly more primitive as we move further into the past. In reality, however, it seems to be just the opposite, destroying today's uniformitarian evolutionary assumptions. Thus, these OOPArts are usually avoided by the media and are almost always hidden from the general public, but the truth must be told.

I will now show you some more examples. Recently, rock hounds in the Coso mountains of California, when examining geodes, discovered an ancient electrical device resembling a spark plug within the geode. The formation of geodes takes very long spans of time. This device may therefore be thousands of years old. I observed a history program on television that showed that a scale model of a very sophisticated airplane was found in an Ancient Egyptian tomb at Saqqara, having been dated at about 200 BC but may be older. Some scholars may think it's a bird, I don't know. So if this is true, then remember that. Every model has a corresponding working prototype. So I wonder how this advanced, ancient airplane—if it is one—was kept secret from posterity? According to the National Science Foundation, an analog computing device with approximately seventy cogged or differential gears—which is more complicated than a modern Swiss watch—dating back to before the time of Christ (the first century BC) was salvaged. It was discovered and recovered in an ancient ship, possibly Greek, in the Aegean Sea; so ancient man had complicated machinery and engineering skills many centuries ago. Artifacts discovered in a grave in Colombia, estimated to be about one thousand years old, could well represent an ancient jet fighter aircraft. These ancient artifacts have wings and a tail structure almost exactly identical to modern military aircraft. Ancient records from India describe aircrafts. The ancient Nazca people of Peru created artwork that can only be observed from aircraft, and the Mayans used observatories. So it appears ancient man understood aerodynamics. According to Henry Waint of the Creation Research Society, in the Mayan city of Copan, an ancient stone carving resembling a modern machine with gears having spoked wheels was discovered. In Costa Rica, hundreds of giant basalt balls were discovered, weighing sixteen tons each. Only advanced high-precision tools or machinery could have made them. They are very old and of unknown origin and purpose in Bosnia larger ones were found. Electric batteries have been found in some ancient Babylonian and Minoan cities. Now new evidence has been recently brought to light. Because of recent excavations, it has been found that the ancient Egyptians may have used their own version of light bulbs in the ancient tombs where torches would not work properly because of the low oxygen content. Consequently, ancient man used electricity. According to the History Channel, pyramids are found not only in Egypt and Mexico. There is a pyramid belt dating back to around four to five thousand years ago circling around the world. Amazingly, the Egyptian Pyramid of Khufu and the Mexican Pyramid of the Sun have perimeters that are exactly the same size: 750 square feet. These amazing similarities may well prove that either the ancient architects received this knowledge from the Tower of Babel or that trade could have existed between both nations after the same technical source before the tower was destroyed and mankind was scattered (refer to chapter 4). According to Homer, during this period, the ancient Greek Hephaestus built complicated working robots many centuries before the modern science of robotics was born. I believe that when we investigate the past, we are exploring the future. The reason for this is that our human history always works in mathematically predictable cycles and constantly repeats itself. During the nineteenth and twentieth centuries and especially now, in the beginning of the twenty-first century, so it appears that scientists are rediscovering technology that was invented many centuries ago. Truly, history teaches us that much of what we as modern-age people take for granted is derived originally from the engineering wonders of the mysterious ancient world. However, most people living today do not realize this fact because they are too busy or too lazy to research and discover the absolute truth.

As you can well imagine, there are many more OOPArts that are now becoming available for both historical and scientific research because secrets always get out. However, I promise to keep this book as brief as is now possible with the knowledge at hand as of AD 2022. So I very strongly recommend that the truly motivated, open-minded students who are intrigued by the information in this unusual chapter continue to explore this subject. Your future outlook on life may depend upon it. The truth is out there. For that reason, never give up your research.

Truly, there are clear indications that the book of Genesis is the basis for truth and that ancient man understood science and nature and was highly advanced, not primitive, having had technical and scientific knowledge possibly even equal to or even greater that our own modern achievements of today. By now, students reading this book are possibly wondering just what happened to all that ancient knowledge or how it was lost in antiquity. It is generally believed that much of this advanced scientific and technical knowledge was lost when the Romans burned down the Great Library of Alexandria in Egypt during Caesar's campaign. We can only imagine what was stored there. Modern researchers can now believe that high officials who were members of secret societies such as the Medieval Knights Templar and the modern-day Bilderbergers may have preserved much of the lost ancient knowledge and kept it classified until information leaked out to the public. However, that has not been proven. It is now believed some secrets concerning ancient technology may possibly have been carefully guarded for centuries by these privileged, self-appointed guardians of knowledge. Also, the old Vatican archives may have some ancient knowledge. Can you find more? They believe knowledge is power just like Eve. Now are you surprised? Remember that real power only comes from faith and submission to Christ. There's only one way (John 4)!

So the overwhelming evidence proves that throughout our recorded human history, mankind was never primitive! Obviously, the Genesis account is true, so any sincere historians must accept this obvious fact and begin teaching the truth. We have the truth, so we who are teachers can no longer avoid this great responsibility. Students have been brainwashed long enough! Now we must reform our universities, colleges, and public schools. We must stop teaching evolution. Now the truth must be told. Dr. D. Chittick stated that "we have seen the evolutionary picture for the origin of man does not match the evidence. The study of human artifacts does not fit with historical evidence. A better picture is needed." I agree with him. The student must be knowledgeable of the incredible fact that from the moment of creation and throughout human history, mankind was always advanced and civilized. The evidence cannot be ignored! So it is obvious to any true scholar that the secular textbooks are wrong. I hope all my readers and students will never stop discovering more examples than those that I have. Truly, the answer to our past as well as our present and future is found in Genesis (Luke 8:17, 12:2).

STUDENT'S NOTES

THE DELUGE OF NOAH

CHAPTER 3

The Deluge of Noah

IN OUR NEW age of secular postmodernism, there is a growing number of scientists and historians who believe that there is strong geological and historical evidence found everywhere that Earth had undergone a universal catastrophic flood. So possibly, as a result, more geologists, teachers, and students are now investigating the true biblical account of the deluge. The deluge is tangible proof that catastrophism, not uniformitarianism, is the correct scientific method.

Chapters 6 through 8 of Genesis contain the exciting account of the deluge of Noah and the ark. It was a necessity for Noah and his family to build the ark. This was based on God's warning of His coming judgment because of man's sin. Remember that God is holy and cannot allow sin in His presence (read Habakkuk 1:13). This time, man went too far! In Genesis 6:5–6, we read that mankind was so evil that God had repented that He had made man. Every thought of mankind was evil continually. Today our world is very close to that condition (Luke 17:26). My students and readers may ask or wonder why only Noah was righteous enough to build the ark and survive the flood. It is a true fact that all of mankind are sinners (Rom. 3:23); however, compared to the out-of-control, rebellious lifestyles of the violent, perverse, and horribly wicked and rebellious world about him, Noah found grace and was blameless before God. So in spite of the possibility of ridicule, Noah faithfully obeyed God, warned people about God's approaching judgment, and built the ark. As a result of his faith and obedience, he and his immediate family were saved. This did not include his large extended family. Although there is no way to establish an exact date, we do know the flood came approximately 120 years after God's warning of His approaching judgment for sin (Genesis 6:3). Nobody listened. We owe our existence to the fact that Noah demonstrated great faith to believe God all those years ago. Although historical records have been changed all over the world to hide the important biblical facts, we still find more than ample archaeological evidence for the Genesis flood supporting the Bible and creation (chapter 7).

The evidence for the deluge is all around us. To start, I'll provide some examples. In Earth's vast oceans, there have been discovered many submerged or sunken cities that are possibly even much older than the ancient cities of Mesopotamia, providing powerful evidence of the Genesis flood. The oldest trees worldwide are approximately four or five thousand years old, proving that they sprouted from seeds planted right after the deluge. It is believed that because of a lack of sunlight and atmosphere, the trees before the flood were drowned and destroyed. Also, according to respected scientist P. Lalondes's research, "about 85% of the rock's surface around the world is made up of sedimentary rock indicating that some time in the past, the world was covered by water." Liberal professors hide this awakening truth.

Gods word is true but some people may doubt so many. Many theologians believe that before the flood, it had never rained (Genesis 2:6). Also, there is a strong possibility that meat was never consumed until after the flood (Genesis 2:16, 9:1–5). God's Word is always true, read the bible despite man's assumptions. The weather conditions and diet of mankind before the flood may be responsible for the long life spans. I will expound more on this topic in chapter 5. Old Testament experts Daniel Ward and H. H. Healy teach us that the time from Adam to the flood was approximately 1,656 to 2,262 years. This allows sufficient time for millions of people to inhabit the entire Earth. However, everywhere that mankind lived, sin was rampant.

In Genesis 6:1–8, we read about the cause and effect of man's sin. This was the reason God brought a flood upon all of Earth. Yet God demonstrated His love and mercy to mankind through Noah.

Chapter 6 of genesis opens with the account of the sons of God and the daughters of man having physical relations, producing men of renown. Only God is to be worshipped or renowned (Exodus 20:3–6). As to the identity of the sons of God, there are many opinions and explanations. Some theologians may believe this refers to the true worshippers or believers in God, who existed during this time in history. Bible historian Victor Hamilton suggests that they are the sons of Seth and the daughters of Cain. Others believe the sons of God refer to fallen angels (demons) who tried to prevent the birth of God's Messiah by polluting the gene pool. In Job 1:6, there is a reference to the sons of God meeting to give an account to God. Satan came also among them. Who they were is not as important as the results of their marriage to the daughters of man. This only increased the wickedness of man. Man's heart was evil continually, and God repented that He had made man. In those days, violence was spreading everywhere. This is what brought on the judgment against sin known as the deluge. Only Noah found grace as he did not conform to society but obeyed God (Hebrews 11:13, 1 Peter 1:8).

One of Noah's ancestors, Enoch, was a man of tremendous faith in God. He was born about 622 years after Adam (Hebrews 11:5, Jude 14–15). In Genesis 5:24, Enoch was taken up to heaven without dying. In Scripture, Genesis 5 and Hebrews 11 state that Enoch was translated, or taken by God. There are often questions as to what this means as well as many opinions. But I personally believe that he ascended to heaven like Jesus did. Yet he inherited Adam's sinful nature, so he must die someday (Romans 6:23). Maybe he will be one of the two witnesses in Revelation 11:1–12. Only Enoch and Elijah entered heaven without dying (2 Kings 2). Enoch must have been skilled in the arts of spiritual living and totally surrendered to the lordship of God. This was not easy to do in those violent, wicked days before the flood, just like the modern world today. The word *equinox* was possibly derived from the name Enoch. He was on Earth for 365 years, just like the days in a year on Earth. The bible says do not fear 365 times. The Bible teaches us the words *do not fear*, which are listed 365 times.

According to the Genesis account in chapter 6, verses 17 to 22, and chapter 7, verses 2 through 5, Noah was commanded by God to preserve mating pairs of every living creature on Earth even skunks. Most modern historians and scientists do not accept the book of Genesis as truth, based upon the fact that they see it as impossible to preserve all those animals, insects, and birds together on one ship. Of every animal considered clean, seven pairs, and of every animal considered unclean, two pairs, two by two, the male and his female, entered the ark. During Noah's time, Kosher laws probably did not exist, so students may assume that laws were in effect then or that clean animals were those used for sacrifice; therefore, a larger number were needed to be preserved. After surviving the flood, Noah sacrificed many clean animals to God. So let us examine the ark and see if it is possible for Noah to transport all those animals. God's Word is true all the time (Romans 3:4).

God gave Noah specific instructions as to how to build the ark. It was to be a ship three hundred cubits long, fifty cubits wide, and thirty cubits high (Genesis 6:15). It was to have three decks. As evidenced by its dimensions, the ark was of a rectangular, flat-bottom construction. Modern twenty-first-century shipbuilders believe concerning Noah's ark that its length-to-width ratio of six-to-one provided excellent buoyancy, strength, and stability on flood waters or high seas. So it would have been almost impossible to turn it over or sink it. Based upon information found in the Gilgamesh epic, author Ralph Pederson concludes that Noah's ark would most likely have been sewn together using ancient techniques preserved today in the Arab world and India. However, I do not share Mr. Pederson's opinion on ark technology. Noah could not have been a primitive man but had to have highly advanced technology in order to build such a large ship. So Mr. Pederson's opinion does not hold water. Noah used hard gopher wood to build the ark. He did not use bulrushes or reeds, which can be sewn together. Also, during the construction process, Noah might have hired many engineers, inspectors, suppliers, craftsmen, and carpenters. So Mr. Pederson is absolutely wrong! By now, many interested students and also my rather curious readers are probably wondering just how large Noah's ark was. Let's examine the available data and find out. A cubit measures about eighteen inches—the average distance from a man's elbow to his fingertips. But a sacred cubit is three feet long. Based on a small cubit, the ark would have been about 437 to 450 feet long, 75 feet wide, and 45 feet high. To allow the student to have a better understanding of this, consider that the ark was about the same size as a Casa Blanca class aircraft carrier in World War II. So the ark weighed possibly thirty-four thousand tons. That's one very large ship!

Now students will often ask the question regarding what kind of wood the gopher wood is that was used to build the ark. My present research has narrowed it down to either cedar or acacia wood; I am guessing but until the ark is recovered, only God, Noah, and his immediate family have the correct answer. Many scholars choose acacia.

Getting back to how the ark was able to transport all those animals and supplies, it is important to remember that our loving God only provided the ark for the preservation of land-dwelling animals and mankind. The students must also consider these facts. According to Dr. K. Seagreaves, who is the author of *The Great Dinosaur Mistake*, it has been calculated that the total number of animals were about thirty-five thousand. So the space needed to carry the animals would be about 146 railcars. The number of insects—about 1,700,000— would fill twenty-one railroad boxcars. The ark was large enough to contain over 522 railroad cars. This leaves room enough for one year's supply of tools, fresh water, wine, food, medicine, and also room for Noah's family. Most students today who know this truth and wisely accept these facts can no longer dismiss the so-called story of the ark as a fairy tale. Genesis 6:14 says that the ark was to be pitched within and then without, with pitch similar to modern tar, asphalt, caulk, or varnish. Teacher and *A Bible Study on Genesis* author V. R. Benson teaches us that the Hebrew word for pitch is the same word used to describe atonement. Truly, the men of Noah's time were highly advanced. A ship this large would not have been necessary for a local flood. The deluge was a universal, or worldwide, flood (Hebrews 11:7). It may seem that almost every time historians and theologians gather together to discuss the deluge, someone may be present who believes in a local flood. But when we consider the size of the ark and the number of animals it carried, the flood had to be universal, or worldwide. Also, one must consider that God's purpose for the flood was to destroy all of sinful and rebellious humanity. This could never have been accomplished by a local flood (Genesis 6:7). And a local flood cannot account for the seashells, limestone deposits, and marine fossils found in inland rock layers on Earth. The Grand Canyon was carved by the Flood.

One thing that has always interested me is the fact that Noah and his family must have had very strong noses! The pungent odor of animal waste must have kept them busy shoveling. No one living today has a real understanding of what conditions were like on the ark. According to journalist Rene Noormberg, Noah was able to maintain an accurate and detailed diary of events even though he and his family were completely shut up in the ark for the first forty days, without any natural means of keeping time (Genesis 8:12). Expert journalist Rene Noormberg believes that this indicates that Noah might have possessed an artificial device to measure time. He also believes that the window in the roof of the ark could not have provided enough sunlight. He suggests that Noah might have had some form of artificial lighting. I believe that Noah and his family must have had various forms of music and entertainment as well as what people of his generation considered to be the comforts of home. Noah might have even carried various types of technology with him on the ark to enable his family to survive in a destroyed environment and harsh climate changes after the flood. But for now, the living conditions on the ark must remain a rather baffling mystery.

As I previously mentioned in the academic survey, the Genesis account of the deluge has many similarities to the ancient Mesopotamian Gilgamesh epic. This has caused many historians to believe that Moses borrowed this information when he wrote Genesis. There are many accounts, however, of a worldwide flood from many cultures and peoples from all around the world. These flood stories that always describe the same devastating, catastrophic event are universal! The ancient Greeks had a universal flood story with amazing similarities to the biblical account. The ancient traditions of the British Islands, India, and China speak of a time when the ancient world was destroyed by a flood. The Romans had a flood tradition preserved by the Latin poet Ovid. The Mexican historian Ixtlilxochitl taught that the Toltecs believed the First World lasted 1716 years, then it was destroyed by a flood that covered the highest mountains. The Benua-Jakum people of the Malay Peninsula believe that the ground is a skin covering the water. They believe that in ancient times, God broke up this skin so that the old world was destroyed by a great flood, the deluge. Also, just like the Genesis account, the Polynesian flood tradition speaks of only eight survivors (Noah's family). Famous researcher Bruce Masse stated that all native American tribes have a universal flood tradition very similar to the Genesis account. The German scholar Dr. Andree has compiled eighty-eight different flood traditions from cultures around the world. History Channel celebrity Bruce Masse stated on television that there are over one hundred flood stories. My personal research has confirmed that there are possibly over two hundred deluge accounts on a worldwide basis read Noah's Ark by Henri Nessen. As Noah's descendants spread out over the world, they took the original deluge account with them. As the information was handed down from generation to generation, the information was changed. The Gilgamesh epic, possibly written during the time of the Jewish patriarchs, is just such a striking example.

God's version is true. The older a story becomes, the more difficult it is for man to believe it. Shamefully, today, in our century, it is easier for modern man to believe in Santa, the Easter Bunny, leprechauns, space aliens, and evolution than accept the obvious and well-documented existing truth concerning the deluge. As it was stated in an earlier chapter on origins, human nature is a fallen nature o due to the original sin. Mankind often questions the truth. Man will use poetic license, adding to or subtracting from the original historical account.

However, God cannot lie. The Lord Jesus referred to the ancient historical biblical account of the deluge recorded by Moses as being the absolute truth (Matthew 24:37–39, Revelation 22:19).

Many Bible teachers may refer to the ark as the first zoo. Truly, this was God's perfect version of wildlife conservation. All the genetic diversity in nature, both in humans and animals, was preserved on the ark so that God could receive the glory. In Genesis 6:9, we read that Noah was perfect in his generations. Every known type, race, ethnicity or nationality of mankind descended from Noah and his family. Therefore, we are all related. DNA evidence has proven this fact. This passage of Scripture also implies that all in Noah's direct line of ancestors worshipped God. It's our sinful nature that prevents us from acting like one big happy family.

By now many of you are probably asking, "What happened to the dinosaurs?" After all, there is, according to most textbooks, an extinct possibility that dinosaurs are still living today! I believe Noah had dinosaurs and, not surprisingly, also unicorns present with him on the ark (Job 39:9). Remember that God commanded Noah to preserve every kind of animal including dinosaurs. In the book of Job, chapters 40 and 41, we read about dinosaur-like creatures such as the massive behemoth that had a tail as large as a Cedar tree trunk as well as other possible dinosaurs that existed after the flood. In our past history, there are many stories of dragons, which may have been dinosaurs (Psalm 148:7, Jeremiah 51:37, Malachi 1:3). Both human and dinosaur footprints have been found together in Glen Rose (Texas, USA) and other places on Earth, offering proof that humans and dinosaurs existed together not too long ago. Also, according to the Inca cultural expert Dr. Cabrara, ancient artwork in Peru and Colombia depict humans and dinosaurs coexisting after the deluge. The *mokele-mbembe* is a creature that some scientists believe could be a surviving sauropod-type dinosaur, perhaps similar to a brontosaurus, living in the rivers of the Congo or Cameroon. There have been numerous reports of teresaurus living deep in the remote jungles of New Guinea and in Arizona, U.S.A. (Thunderbirds). Also, many animals living today such as Scotland's famous Nessie, the Loch Ness Monster, and the unusual Komodo dragon can be classified as dinosaurs.

There is strong evidence to support the idea that Neanderthals developed as a result of the deluge. Today, the majority of modern twenty-first-century historians and scientists believe that the Neanderthal man was not a missing link but just as human as you or I and with larger brains. They followed religious practices, built shelters, used sophisticated tools, and even buried their dead. Nearly one hundred years ago, skeleton expert Dr. Virchau and, about fifty years ago, Dr. A. J. E. Cave diagnosed arthritis and rickets in the famous Neanderthal bones, accounting for their apelike or primitive appearance (see *Big Daddy* by Chick). During this time, just after the flood, the strong possibility of reduced sunlight from volcanic ash, the lack of proper medicines and fruit, and the lack of seafood would incline individuals to a vitamin D deficiency, leading to rickets. So the harsh conditions after the flood of Noah may have been the cause of Neanderthalism. For students, this is a hypothesis worth consideration. Also, it is a well-established and proven scientific fact that the longer people live or the greater they age, the more Neanderthal in appearance their bones become. Remember, people lived very long lives during the time of Noah. Perhaps they are the fascinating but mysterious Neanderthals.

The deluge began after Noah's entire immediate family had boarded the ark. Then it continued to rain everywhere on Earth for forty days and forty nights, destroying all of sinful mankind. Once God closed the door to the ark, man's salvation became impossible. They never listened to or obeyed Noah's warning about God's approaching judgment. They acted just like people living today (John 3:16, Matthew 24:38–39). The screams and cries from the evil, unsaved, wicked people and land animals who were left outside the ark must have been horrifying. Only Noah's immediate family survived the deluge. Holy Scripture confirms that there were only eight people to repopulate the world.

About 150 days after the flood started, the ark landed in the mountains of Ararat in modern Turkey. Mount Ararat is about 5,156 meters high, so the floodwaters were very deep. Our father, Noah, released some birds every seven days to test the environment. The last bird he sent out was a dove, which returned with an olive branch in its beak. The earth was drying up; however, it was about eight months before God spoke to Noah and his family. Then they released all the animals and moved out of the ark and onto dry land. Noah always waited for God to guide him and never lost his faith. Today the dove and olive branch arc symbols of peace.

In Genesis 9:7–17, we read about God's unconditional covenant with Noah and his descendants (all of humanity) after the flood. God promised never to destroy the whole Earth with another universal flood. The sign of the covenant is the rainbow, demonstrating God's beauty and glory. God said this would be an everlasting covenant, so the rainbow should be an encouragement to all the true believers who look upon it. Unfortunately, some people today use the rainbow as a symbol of tolerance for a life of devastating sexual perversion. However, the rainbow should always remind mankind of God's everlasting mercy and love. The covenant is important because we discover in Genesis 9:18–25 that Noah and his family still had the ability to sin, which they inherited from Adam and Eve. The sin of Noah's son Ham is a prime example of our inherited carnal or sinful nature. Just in case the students are interested, Dr. Richard Riss of Pillar Christian College in New Jersey teaches us that the biblical evidence strongly suggests that the sin of Ham was incest. (Please refer to Deuteronomy 27:20) and Leviticus 20:17). This happened when Noah was drunk and unable to prevent it from happening. In Genesis 9:21–29, brothers Shem and Japheth had to walk backward to cover up their father, Noah's, nakedness. This holy scripture strongly suggests that the act of seeing his father naked was Ham's only sin. Scholars can argue, but God always tells the truth. Author and Bible teacher Victor Hamilton suggests that after the sin of Ham, Noah cursed Canaan because he was Ham's son. After the flood, mankind still needed a Redeemer or Messiah. However, God will honor His covenant with man. The next time God judges man's sin by destroying the whole Earth, it will be by fire. This is found in 2 Peter 3. So be prepared. If my students and readers don't choose to heed this ominous warning, then please consider that our present world now has an enormous stockpile of thermonuclear weapons that are more than capable of accomplishing this future judgment the real big bang (John 3:16, Thessalonians 4:16–18, Zachariah 14:12).

In both recent and past history, there have been many sightings of Noah's ark. Reports from the third century BC suggest that it was common knowledge that the ark of Noah could still be viewed on Mount Ararat. In 290 BC, the renowned wise man Berovsos the Chaldean recorded that many tourists would often visit Noah's ark. He wrote that some of the visitors would take home with them pieces of wood from the ark for good luck charms. According to the famous Jewish historian Josephus, who lived during Roman times, ancient people often went on pilgrimages to see the ark. During World War I, there were sightings over Mount Ararat of what was believed to be the ark by a Russian pilot named Roskovitsky flying over the area. In 1915, just before the Russian Revolution, the czar sent an expedition to Mount Ararat. They found the ark and made detailed records of it. Upon return to Russia, they were captured by the Communists. During the twentieth century, famous explorers Schwingham, Hagopian, and Navarra claimed to have on separate occasions discovered the ark in the vicinity of the Ahora Gorge on Mount Ararat, it's recorded. In the 1930s, Hardwick Knight from New Zealand discovered the ark without knowing it. In 1952, the famous American mining engineer George J. Green took photographs of Noah's ark from a helicopter. In the late 1950s, the well-known explorer Gregor Schwinghammer claimed he had observed the ark of Noah from an E-100 type of aircraft. He described it as a large boxcar lying high upon Mount Ararat. In 1960, a Turkish Army officer named Captain Duripinar, when examining aerial photographs, noticed a large boat-like object upon Mount Ararat at a height of about 6,300 feet; and many people believe this could be Noah's ark. In 1971, noteworthy author and archeologist Dr. John Morris from ICR (the Institute for Creation Research in California, USA) and his team climbed Mount Ararat and claimed to have observed Noah's ark. Chuck Aaron of Florida (USA) photographed the ark on his September 15, 1989, flight over the mountain. These photos are available in the Immanuel Expedition Foundation in Orlando. Today, based upon the Florida photographs and possibly more new sighting reports, it is generally believed that the ark is preserved and resting in two pieces somewhere above the ten-thousand-foot level upon the mountain this is the one discovery New Agers, Darwinists, secular historian, and communists do not want revealed. It destroys evolution.

There are many more accounts of sightings of the ark. So please carefully consider the evidence presented in this chapter. Obviously, the biblical account of Noah and the ark are true; and therefore, as a result, so are you, me, and everyone else living on the Earth. So honest professors are responsible for teaching the truth. Remember that without Noah's ark, we who are teachers would have no history to teach or students to benefit from our knowledge. I personally would like someday to have the opportunity to go on an expedition to rediscover and recover the ark. However, with the present religious plotting, secrets, and money grabbers as well as the deep state and political conditions and socialism prevailing in the world, it may be too difficult to accomplish. The evil world religions can prevent it from happening. But truly, everything will be done in God's timing and according to His perfect will. Let's give God the glory (Psalm 150)! The truth will set you free (John 8:32). The ark will be found and recovered.

STUDENT'S NOTES

THE TOWER OF BABEL

CHAPTER 4

The Tower of Babel

THE TOWER OF Babel is one of the most recognized focal points in our human history, linking together every nation, people, religion, and language group back to one common beginning. However, there has been a lot of controversy among historians and scientists as to whether there was a tower and whether man was really of one race and spoke the same language before the tower (Acts 17:26). This could become a baffling issue. Yet modern DNA research has proven that all of mankind's lineage can be traced back to one common origin. We all descended from Adam and Eve (refer to chapter 1). Historian Victor Hamilton, basing his view on the genealogy of Shem, believes there was possibly more than one language during the time of the Tower of Babel. I disagree with him. Truly, the Holy Scripture is clear that all of mankind had only one language before the Tower of Babel was destroyed (Genesis 11:1–9). So to explain man's diversity, we must discover when the Tower of Babel was constructed and what purpose it served. The following paragraphs will deal with this question. The tower is believed by some theologians to have been constructed about 101 to 126 years after the deluge, but this is debatable. Other scholars believe that construction began about 530 or 870 years after the deluge of Noah. I will provide more information on possible resources and dates of the tower's construction in my time line (last chapter). Too many scholars disagree on this topic.

In Genesis 11, we read that the descendants of Noah traveled from the east toward the land of Shinar, or Mesopotamia, and settled there. This is very significant to modern historians because many theologians can mistakenly believe they traveled south, directly from Noah's ark on Mount Ararat to Babel in the Tigris-Euphrates valley. But that's not east of Shinar, and since God's word is true, they must have first settled east of Mount Ararat and Mesopotamia. According to archaeologist F. Mackey, it has been discovered that there are ancient settlements along the Indus River Valley that are possibly far older that the ancient cities of Mesopotamia (modern-day Iraq). They are called Mohenjo-Daro and Harappa. These settlements may have existed as far back as 3500 to 3000 BC. Thus, when Noah's descendants traveled from the east, it might have been from these important ancient settlements.

Now, as we look back at Genesis 11, in reference to our ancestors (Noah's descendants), the Scripture states that they said to one another, "Let us build a city and a tower whose top may reach unto heaven, and let us make us a name lest we be scattered abroad upon the face of the whole earth." But God, in His perfect wisdom, commanded them to scatter around the earth (Genesis 9:1). Remember, they were building a tower whose top would reach heaven. Perhaps they wanted to reach up to God. Many theologians believe that the Tower of Babel was built as a symbol for religious rebellion against God and a center for occult practices. There is also the possibility that they did not believe the promise God made to them in Genesis 9:11–17 and wanted to be high enough to escape another devastating flood. They might have wanted a center of commerce for a world economy and one-world government. Today, through tolerance of sin and socialism, modern man is trying to establish a new world order (Revelation 6:3–4). Researcher, author, and Bible scholar V. R. Benson teaches us that they wanted to make a tower so they could use it to worship the heavens. History author Victor Hamilton teaches us that the Tower of Babel was a symbol of pagan immortality. There are many variables concerning the reason for the Tower of Babel. One or more may be correct. But we may be certain that the tower was dedicated to the glory of man.

Dr. D. Chittick of George Fox College believes that the tower might have been designed as an observatory to view astronomical objects. I tend to agree with him; however, I suggest that there might have been much more involved. It might have been a place to keep records and develop new technology (Genesis 11:6). As I stated in chapter 2, there is evidence that ancient man was far more advanced than most of the modern history books have recorded. The scientific and technical achievement of early mankind as one unified body could have become very impressive and perhaps quite dangerous. The tower might have been designed for astrology. Both Drs. Chittick and Alexander Hislop, who wrote the famous book *The Two Babylons*, imply in their enlightening books that astrology was well established before the people were scattered. Also, ancient peoples all over the world had an amazing knowledge of the stars and planets. Much of this knowledge might have been taken from knowledge established when the Tower of Babel was in use. Many cultures and peoples shared much of the same technical knowledge, yet they were living great distances apart. So I believe they might have received this knowledge from the same source: the Tower of Babel. Amazingly, many different cultures all around the world possessed the same musical knowledge and diatonic and pentatonic scales as well as similar musical instruments such as various forms of flutes, drums, horns, and harps. Again, this phenomenon suggests that music originated from one original source. For more information, read *The God-Kings & Titans* by James Bailey, an excellent book.

God's perspective is the best way to understand our purpose and history. Let's examine it. We read in Genesis 11 that all of mankind was of one speech and language. So in a state of rebellion or sin, the Tower of Babel was constructed so man could make a name for himself, giving glory to man, not God. Then, with anger, God responded by confusing their languages, which resulted in mankind being scattered all over the earth. Many linguists today believe that all languages descended from one original source. In fact, famous Greek historian Plato wrote about an ancient golden age of man when everyone spoke the same language. According to Bible history professors Dillard and Longman, when man's communication became impossible, then man's rebellion or sin as one unified body was impossible. This was accomplished so that God could work out His wonderful salvation plan through one chosen people: the nation of Israel (refer to chapter 6).

There are many related accounts of the tower in folklore around the world. A good example is that the Aztecs of Mexico have a story about a great pyramid constructed at Cholula specially designed to protect them from future floods. The ancient Greek historian Abydenus wrote about a great high tower in Babylon that was destroyed by the gods who then confounded the original language of all mankind. The Babylonian account translated by George Smith of the British Museum states that the building of the temple offended the gods. In a night, they threw down what had been built, scattered them around, and made strange their speech. According to the Mexican historian Ixtlilxochitl, the Toltecs believed that after a worldwide flood, men erected a high tower to take refuge in, but their language was confusing and they moved to different parts of the earth. This is similar to the Genesis account. The list above is brief because I intend to make this book brief. However, I encourage students to find more examples.

It is believed that many of the towers, pyramids, ziggurats, and temples found in ancient cities could well be reproductions or versions of the original Tower of Babel. In our recent history, the Twin Towers of the World Trade Center were constructed as a center of commerce. It might have been similar in purpose to the Tower of Babel in regard to being a center for a one-world global economy. The late great David Wilkerson, a famous preacher of Times Square Church in New York City, teaches us that God allows the destruction of our symbols of prosperity (such as the mighty World Trade Center towers) because that's where we place our pride and reliance. I agree with him. God should be our high tower (Psalm 144:2, Jeremiah 6:27). Someday we will discover the truth concerning these things. Many tower-type structures have been built around the world so sinful man can make a name for himself, glorifying man, not God.

Some modern theologians believe that the Tower of Babel may have been constructed during the time of Peleg (Phaleg) who may have lived in approximately 3152 BC or 2222 BC (refer to the time line). Barry Setterfield from Australia dates Peleg as living 530 years after the deluge, or flood, or that the ancient tower was constructed then. In Genesis 10:25 and 1 Chronicles 1:19, we read that in the time of Peleg, the earth was divided. This could mean the people were divided or scattered and that their language was divided as well. However, according to British scientist Author Bill Cooper of the Creation Science movement and Dr. Chittick from George Fox College, the word *divided* translated from the original Hebrew means "to measure," not "to scatter." In his shocking book, historian J. Bailey presents tangible evidence that the ancient Mesopotamians had already measured and circumnavigated the globe thousands of years before St. Brendan, Magellan, Drake, or Columbus. In fact, ancient Welsh poetry illustrates what appears to be these exciting voyages. So the ancient world was indeed measured. According to James Bailey and others, trade existed among early civilizations. It is now believed that the plants used for mummification in Egypt came from Peru and that artifacts from Mesopotamia were discovered in Mexico, accounting for very similar construction projects, etc. Also, ancient Ecuadorian and Egyptian artwork display amazing similarities, as does the artwork of ancient Mexico and Nepal.

Archaeology expert C. Berlitz teaches us that ancient world travelers drew maps of America more than 2,500 years ago. Some of their maps have been recovered and are available today. This is available, tangible proof that the ancient world was measure long, long ago. However, Rabbi Tietz of the Jewish Education Center in Elizabeth, New Jersey, translates this passage to mean "disperse" or "scatter." This interpretation is supported and widely accepted by a large number of Hebrew language scholars and is the view of this author. I believe it means the people were scattered. Dr. Hislop believes that the Tower of Babel was constructed during the time of Nimrod or shortly before his time. Many modern scientists, historians, and teachers who study plate tectonics believe that the continents of the world were all joined together. So many pastors, scholars, and students are also interested. Many people assume that during Peleg's time, they were divided. Because of the great longevity of people during that time, it is possible that Peleg and Nimrod were contemporaries. Perhaps they even knew each other. The name Peleg probably means "to disperse," "to scatter," or "to divide." Also, Peleg may be translated as Babel or Babeler, depending on translation.

Most people today recognize the name Nimrod as being associated with the Tower of Babel. In the Aggadah, we read that the rabbis called the Tower of Babel the House of Nimrod. According to both biblical and secular records, Nimrod is believed to have established the first empire and a one-world government system centered around the city and Tower of Babel (refer to Genesis 10:8–12, the Gilgamesh epic, and *The Two Babylons*). Nimrod was known as the mighty hunter. The Jewish Talmud states that he was a hunter of the souls of men. According to Dr. Hislop in his book *The Two Babylons*, evidence was discovered describing Nimrod a descendant of Cush. He might have been Black and is often pictured in publications wearing a horn, but we cannot be certain. Horns have been used as a symbol to represent nations and empires (Daniel 7, Revelation 13:1). In the *Encyclopedia of Freemasonry*, Nimrod is referred to as one of the founders of masonry. According to Dr. Hislop and most scholars, King Nimrod has been associated with or identified as the Babylonian god Marduk, or Nebo; the Canaanite god Moloch; and the constellation Orion. Dr. A. Hislop believes that the Mesopotamian, Greek, Roman, and Egyptian pantheon of gods was originally derived from Nimrod and his wife Semiramis. Queen Semiramis has sometimes in Ancient Egypt been associated with the star Sirius; and she was known in many ancient cultures as the Queen of Heaven, Earth Mother, Holy Mother, Isis, Shing Moo, Diana, Venus, Ashtoreth Devaki, or Mother Goddess. In reference to Semiramis, author and researcher Ian Wilson in his book *Before the Flood* wrote that a large number of ancient civilizations worshipped a female goddess. People still worship her today, she is often depicted wearing blue (Jer:44). The future evil world leader or Antichrist may be considered the second Nimrod, especially if we who are Bible history teachers continue to allow neo-Darwinism to be taught in our schools! Nimrod means "Let us rebel." Gilgamesh might actually be Nimrod (Revelation 16:13–16, 19:11–21).

I believe that writing might have come about as a result of the confusing of tongues at the Tower of Babel. When people could no longer communicate verbally with one another, they had to develop an alternate mode of communication for history, business, and commerce. According to British archaeologist Sir Lenard Woolley, "All archaeological evidence seems to prove that writing was first developed in southern Mesopotamia." The Sumerians invented cuneiform writing possibly around 3500 BC after the deluge and Tower of Babel. So the confusion of tongues might well have been the cause of writing, revolutionizing the way we keep historic records and thus enabling us to have the book of Genesis. In my astute opinion, no other invention can surpass the importance of writing. Truly, writing allowed mankind to communicate over long distances and even throughout the ages.

According to Zarephath professor of biblical studies Professor Hagg's research, there seems to be no evidence of writing before the time of Uruk 3. This city might have been constructed shortly after the tower, possibly 3300 or 2800 BC. But we cannot be certain of the date. Some archaeologists believe that a form of writing or record keeping might have been developed in the Indus River Valley at about the same time that writing was developed in (Shinar) Mesopotamia or shortly before that time. Many historians believe this. However, explorer Sir L. Woolley believes it is highly probable that the Indus River Valley owes its writing to Mesopotamia. Renowned author Dr. H. Morris of the Institute for Creation Research in California, USA, dates the beginning of writing at about 3500 to 2002 BC after the Tower of Babel and during the first Egyptian dynasty (hieroglyphics). Note that later in history, first the Phoenicians and then the Jews and Greeks invented the alphabet, improving writing techniques. The information in this book is subject to an update as more discoveries are made and pertinent information becomes available. Unfortunately, less than 10 percent of the records of antiquity are available to us. It's up to the archeologists to discover the more relevant artifacts; however, they are strange working people with odd jobs because their business is in ruins (refer to chapter 7).

As to the actual location of the Tower of Babel, it is believed to have been constructed in the city of Babylon. Both the Temple of Nebo and the Antiochus Cylinder (Tongue Tower) and the ancient temple of Etemn-An-Ki have been proposed as possible sites of the tower. Polyhistor's ancient history places the Tower of Babel in the north side on the city. Historical records reveal that the Greek historian Herodotus visited King Nebuchadnezzar's reconstructed version of the Tower of Babel in 460 BC and was very impressed. The reconstructed tower was believed to have been built upon the foundation of the original tower; however, this account does not provide us with a place or location within the city walls. The construction of the ancient city or the original Tower of Babel was never completed, and so many centuries have gone by since its construction that it is very difficult to be certain just where the tower was located. This is very important because recently, attempts have been made to restore the city and, therefore, perhaps plans to rebuild the tower. Perhaps future archaeological discoveries will solve this puzzling ancient mystery.

Babylon or Babel, located about fifty or sixty miles from modern-day Baghdad, between the Tigris and Euphrates rivers, was for many centuries the wonder city of the ancient world. There were 250 towers and one hundred gates of brass as well as large tunnels, ferry boats, bridges, gardens, and huge temples, just like many modern cities today. New York is a modern type of Babylon (Swaggart, *Study Bible*). Perhaps much of mankind's origins and culture had their beginnings there. Unfortunately, few people living today realize the great significance of the ancient tower throughout our folklore and violent human history. The infamous but influential Tower of Babel truly was the symbol of man's glory. I believe that no other structure on Earth has had such a powerful impact upon man's history, culture, language, and religion than the notorious Tower of Babel. In fact, we can still observe the true and obvious results all around us today. In respect to one of the proposed original locations, some famous archaeologists, theologians, and history authors and professors believe that another name for the Tower of Babel (depending on the translator) is Etemenanki, meaning "the house of the foundations of heaven and earth, whose top reaches to heaven."

STUDENT'S NOTES

THE TABLE OF NATIONS

CHAPTER 5

The Table of Nations

THE BIBLICAL ACCOUNT known as the Table of Nations is located in Genesis 10–11. It teaches us all about Biblical genealogies, diversity, and our ancient ancestors. It's an exciting adventure when we can trace our lineage back to Noah and then to Adam. This proves that mankind has a moral responsibility to God, who created us. The more we know about our ancestors, the more meaningful our lives become. We were all specially created in the image of God. But my personal observations have confirmed that those students who sincerely believe they evolved from apes will have a much greater tendency to act like apes! Origins always affect moral behavior. However, human remains have been found in older rock formations as compared to the remains of the presumed hominid ancestors of man. Johanson's Australopithecus, Lucy, is one of the oldest-known presumed ancestors of humans. It is believed by evolutionists to be 2.9 million years old. However, world-famous archeologist Richard Leakey's wife found a normal human skull under rock dated by evolutionists to be 212 million years old. The evidence proves that mankind is older than our presumed hominid ancestors. So evolution never happened. Hominids never existed. It's just more of Darwin's monkey business. Don't let this discovery surprise you. The Genesis account is true. We all descended from Seth, Noah, and Adam; and all people are responsible to God.

One of the most amazing facts in the Bible is that people before the deluge lived very long lives. Some students find this difficult to accept or believe because this is not the way it is with people living today. However, the evident longevity of ancient man has often caused both wonder and skepticism among students and scholars, with many fascinating but frustrating opinions. Yet the available historical evidence powerfully supports the Genesis account! The tangible evidence is clear that evolution is hearsay and not substantiated at all. So the biblical account is true. The longevity of ancient man, especially the secular king's list, have been recorded diligently in available books by many competent, well-respected, ancient, mostly pagan or secular historians. The list included names such as Ephorus, Manetho, Hecataeus, Josephus, Berosus, Ninshubur, Acusilaus, and Hesiod. Their classic writings are an excellent and powerful testimony to the amazing but true longevity of ancient man. To all my students, this is without any doubt most certainly worth consideration. In Genesis 5:27, it states that Methuselah lived for 969 years. In Genesis 5:5, it says that Adam himself lived for 930 years. In Genesis 9:29, it says that all the days of Noah were 950 years. After the flood, however, the life spans became progressively shorter. In Genesis 11:16–17, it states that Eber lived for 434 years. In Genesis 11:18–19, we read that Peleg lived for 239 years. Genesis 25:7 states that Abraham lived for 175 years, and according to Genesis 50:26, Joseph lived for 110 years. But King David only lived for 70 years. Notice the steady decline. Today, in the beginning of the twenty-first century, a life span of seventy to ninety years is now considered normal (Psalm 90, 2 Peter 3:8). The longer we live, and the more we can accomplish and achieve, so the greater the responsibility we have to God, who wonderfully made us for His glory. So plan wisely and make every moment count.

Some historians and scientists who cannot find an explanation for this amazing longevity may try to explain that years were measured differently in ancient times. One often-used explanation is that a year might have been a full moon or a seasonal change. There is no tangible evidence discovered, however, to support this opinion. As far back as I could research, there was no evidence that a year was basically anything but a twelve-month or approximately 365-day period. Every ancient culture believed this. Remember that God does not lie. The Genesis account is true (Proverbs 3:19).

Many theologians agree with the viewpoint that one of the factors responsible for the ancient longevity of man was the water vapor canopy or hydrosphere surrounding the earth before the Genesis flood. Dr. H. Morris of the Institute of Creation Research (ICR) in California often promoted this school of thought. It is generally believed that this firmament, canopy, or ancient hydrosphere produced a uniform warm temperature around the globe and worked to block out harmful radiation from the Sun. This harmful cosmic gamma radiation can accelerate the aging process. Please read Genesis 1:6–8. Significant age gaps in longevity between Eber and Peleg also might have been caused or affected by extra gamma radiation from massive supernovas, pulsars, and quasars in outer space, often observed in China and Iraq during ancient times. Without the water vapor canopy to protect the earth, this can occur again in our future. There is also the possibility that people living before the Genesis flood might have had less stress, a better diet, and even possibly better medical care than we do today. In Genesis 2–5, we read that after the sins of Adam and Cain, God cursed the ground so it would not produce the same results when we farm it for food. So it is quite possible that our produce or edible plants over the centuries have deteriorated and are presently no longer as potent or life-generating as their ancient varieties were before the curse and the deluge. So our normal diet may be different today, no longer extending our longevity. After all, according to our modern explanation and expectation for our own longevity, it is stated that it's all because of diet, exercise, health care, and genetics. Human aging is a form of entropy (refer to chapter 1).

Other theologians and scholars believe that the shorter life spans after the flood, or deluge, are a direct result of the fall of man and sin. John Wesley believed that man steadily deteriorated and that man's longevity and intellect were diminished after the original sin was committed. Although, it is evident that mankind has been digressing, not evolving, since the devastating fall of mankind. In my astute opinion, the existence of the firmament, hydrosphere or water canopy surrounding the earth in Genesis 1 is the more viable explanation. Remember that it was after the deluge, or flood, when the water vapor canopy was destroyed, not after the fall of man, and the life spans slowly decreased to close to what they are today. Yet man's steady deterioration of his mental abilities since the time of the fall of man may certainly, however, account for the reason so many people blindly believe in evolution (Isaiah 5:21, Romans 1:21–28).

In Genesis 10:1, we discover that all nations of the earth came from Noah and his sons—Shem, Ham, and Japheth. Man's ancient records confirm this truth. Most of the time, secular genealogies found throughout the world will match up almost perfectly with the biblical account. The famous scholar and Englishman Genealogy expert Bill Cooper's book *After the Flood* contains more detailed information. Both the secular and biblical records prove each other to be accurate and reliable. The ancient pagan or secular scholars from antiquity who compiled the genealogies were neither Jewish nor Christian. According to Author Bill Cooper of the Creation Science Movement, they compiled their genealogies long before the Bible was introduced into their countries, yet they came up with the same information that is contained in the book of Genesis. Sadly, the evolutionists always try to hide this astounding, important fact. Just ask them why.

So let's learn about our ancient parents and carefully examine the truth! In Genesis 10:2–5, we read about the sons of Japheth, the son of Noah. They are Gomer, Magog, Madai, Javan, Meshech, Tubal, and Tiras. GOMER is the father of both the Cimmerians and the Germanic peoples. The Germans, French, English, Scandinavians, Italians, Goths, etc. trace their lineage back to him. Also, many Western Europeans have ancient Roman ancestry. According to the expert Bill Cooper MAGOG is believed to be the father of the Galatians, Gaels, Belgae, Scythinians, or Scots. They are the Celtic peoples. The Irish trace their lineage back to him. The Irish are world-renowned saints, musicians, scholars, and poets. Note that this author is Irish. The land referred to in Ezekiel Magog is now modern-day Russia. MADAI is the father of the Medes of the ancient Persian emperor, or the Kurds. Many can debate this, but you can research it. JAVAN is the father of the ancient Greeks, who spread Hellenic culture throughout the known world. TUBAL is the father of some non-Russian Baltic and Slavic peoples. The city Tobolsk is named after him. MESHECH, or MUSKU, is the father of the Russians. The city of Moscow, or Moskva, bears his name. TIRAS is the father of the Thracians, an obscure blue-eyed race. These are the indigenous peoples of Europe today. TOGARMAH may be modern-day Turkey. The people of Spain and Portugal have both European and Semitic roots.

In Genesis 10:6–20, we read about the amazing sons of Ham. They are Cush, Mizraim, Put, and Canaan. CUSH, or KUSH, is the father of the beautiful Sub-Sahara African nations. The land of Cush is Nubia and Ethiopia. The Bantu, Zulu, Igbo, Maasai, Watusi, Dagon, Eubangi Mandan, and Pigmies, etc. are his children. He may also be the father of the peoples of India. The Hindu Kush mountains are in Pakistan, the Polynesians and Abaraidgeines may also be his descendants. Nimrod was the son of Cush. MIZRAIM is the father of the Egyptians and the Philistines. The Hebrew word for *Egypt* preserves this name today. PUT is now believed to be the father of people living in Libya, or Cyrenaica. CANAAN is the father of the Canaanites, who comprise such famous people groups as the Amorites, Hittites, Jebusites, Hivites, and Phoenicians. According to genealogy expert A. Custace, Canaan's son SIN is believed to be the father of the innovative Chinese, who proudly call themselves the Sino people, and the Han (or Ham) Chinese. Most native East Asians are descended from him.

In Genesis 10:21–31, we read about the sons of Shem. They are Elam, Asshur, Arphaxad, Lud, and Aram. ELAM is the father of the Elamites or Haltamti people. They can be believed by some scholars to quite possibly be the Persians. ASSHUR is the father of the Assyrians, who were a major enemy of ancient Israel. ARPHAXAD is the father of the Chaldeans, or Babylonians. His descendants also include Abraham, Isaac, Jacob, Joseph, Judah, David, and the Messiah, the Lord Jesus. All of the history of mankind revolves around the chosen Jewish people or is affected by the lines of Shem and Arphaxad. They are the Semitic peoples. LUD is the father of the Lydians of Asia Minor. ARAM is the father of the Syrians, or Arameans, and related Eastern peoples (refer to Paddan Aram in Genesis 28:2). These are the sons of Noah and a rather brief but accurate description of the Table of Nations, which demonstrate our common lineage, heritage, and origins. I challenge all the sincere and motivated students to make a detailed study of the names listed in this chapter. It is truly amazing just how many ancient and modern cities, countries, and notable places around the world display these names (1 Chronicles 1 and 2). Nations can change their names to hide the truth, and they often do so. But their original names reflect their true biblical origins.

Modern biblical scholarship has developed a concept that is worth examining. It is now believed that only when the phrase "called his name" is used in Scripture does it refer to an immediate descendant. The phrase "called his name" always indicates a father-son relationship. Sometimes biblical names are used as reference points to biblical and historical events and can be used as relevant points of time in Jewish history. Researchers must remember this fact. So biblical genealogies are not always complete family trees. For example, Seth called his name Enos, which is a father-son relationship. Many theologians believe that when this phrase is NOT used, it is a reference to a distant, non-father-son ancestry. The Lord Jesus, for example, is in many places in the Bible referred to as the son of David, emphasizing his Messiahship even though he is not David's immediate son. I hope this concept will allow you to have a much better understanding of the Table of Nations and all of Scripture. The better we understand the Bible, the more we can enjoy reading it to improve our lives (Mathew 1:1). This information will aid pastors, teachers, and students in their understanding of origins, diversity, time lines, Jewish history, and biblical genealogies. Remember, we can always learn from the past.

When the Table of Nations was compiled, the world was a very different place from what it is today, with very different cultures and values. It was vitally important for ancient people to keep an accurate record of their lineage. Free men of prominence knew who their great-grandfathers' were. There are no missing links or transitional forms. To date, they have never been found anywhere on the earth, and they never will be discovered because they do not exist. But evolutionists will continue to disregard the evidence and resume their costly mistakes. In regard to man's origins, the Genesis account, wonderfully supported by strong evidence and available history and artifacts, is trustworthy, reliable, and true (Romans 3:4).

For some Bible scholars including myself, genealogies are fascinating and informative modes for research and Bible study. But some teachers and students may view Genesis 5, 10, and 11 as simply containing long lists of names and rather boring. They haven't discovered the meaning yet. If the readers of this unique book develop an interest, however, in God's wonderful salvation plan and thus are interested in the lineage of the Messiah, these passages of Holy Scripture can become a valuable tool in unlocking the mysteries of the Bible and aid scholars in a serious search for truth. I personally have found that it can be challenging, rewarding, and enjoyable to trace the lineage of the Lord Jesus from Adam to Noah to Abraham to David and finally to Joseph and the Virgin Mary. There are 52 generations from Abraham to the Lord Jesus. (Matt. 1:17).

Remember that the sinister and rather simian false teachings of Darwin are accepted by busy students and teachers without researching or questioning it first, and now it is permeating our modern society. Evolution is dangerous, so the purpose of this enlightening chapter is to provide the reader with insight and inspiration to continue studying God's precious Holy Word and aid the believer with a powerful awareness and truth regarding their origins and ancestors. Very few books will allow you this marvelous privilege. Exploring your past by returning to Genesis will allow you, the seeker of truth, to discover your origins, ancestors, heritage, and future. I hope you enjoyed this chapter regarding your ancestors. History is truly an adventure. We must teach the truth. Darwinism is dangerous. So, always believe the biblical truth. I encourage you to trace your genealogy. I can guarantee, however, that no matter how far you can trace back your family tree, there will most definitely NOT be a monkey swinging from it!

STUDENT'S NOTES

THE PATRIARCHS

CHAPTER 6

The Patriarchs

After the Tower of Babel, God chose a special covenant people to carry out His wonderful salvation plan, designed in a way that all nations would be blessed. God's chosen people are the nation of Israel, or the Jewish people. Refer to Genesis 12–50. The Jewish people were chosen to live holy lives as an example to all nations and give God's Holy Word, the Bible, which included His laws and statutes, to the world. They were also chosen to be God's 144,000 witnesses in the last days (Revelation 7:4). But the most important purpose was to bring forth God's suffering servant, the promised Messiah, the Lord Jesus (Psalm 147:19–20; Psalm 1, 22). The founding fathers of the nation of Israel are known as the patriarchs. They are Abraham, Isaac, Jacob, and Joseph. Their names have great significance when translated from Hebrew into English. Abraham is the "father of a multitude," Isaac is "one laughs," Jacob is "heel grabber or supplanter," and Joseph is "may God add." Their names may reflect both their personalities and how God can chose to deal with them. Names had powerful meanings in those days. Unlike today, a person's name reflected his or her character. Names and titles often changed when lifestyles and purposes changed.

Sometimes, curious students can wonder whether it is possible that Abraham was a contemporary of our father Noah of the flood or deluge fame. Researcher Daniel S. Ward and honored history professor and author Dr. R. Riss confirms that Abraham and Noah were contemporaries. It is believed that Abraham was 58 years old when Noah died at the great old age of 950 years. Author and Bible commentator Dr. L. Richards's writings suggests or wonderfully implies that they might have personally known each other. We do not know.

One of the most reliable methods used to date the time of the patriarchs is achieved by counting backward in history from the Exodus to Abraham. So some students may ask, "Where did they fit into history?" Famous Bible scholars and authors Professors Hill and Walton give two dates for the time of the patriarchs based on accurate times or dates derived by looking back into history from the time of the Exodus. They provided us with an early Exodus date for the Patriarchs of 2166 BC to 1868 or 1805 BC. Based upon a modern controversy, their later Exodus date is 1905 BC to 1650 BC.

In my opinion, a late Exodus date for the patriarchs can present the student with serious problems concerning history. Professor Collins, who is an expert on biblical chronology, provides us with chronological information from an earlier Exodus date for the patriarchs of 2166 or 1951 BC to 1805 or 1806 BC based upon data from the Southwest Institute of Biblical and Theological Studies in New Mexico. This data is from a reliable source (Galatians 3:15–19). I believe that the archaeological and historical evidence now available gives stronger support to use the Hill and Walton and the Southwest Institute early Exodus dates, so I will refer to them in this chapter. This will be as close as I can possibly get to an actual chronology. Bible scholars must continue to research this topic. Maybe you will find more accurate data. Based on the date above, Abraham was either born or called by God in about 2167 BC, and he died in 1992 BC. Isaac was born in about 2067 BC, and he died in 1887 BC. Jacob was born in about 2003 or 1951 BC and died in 1859 or 1726 BC. Joseph was born in about 1915 BC and died in 1805 or 1806 BC. As more information becomes available or important new discoveries are made, these dates may change (refer to the time line in the last chapter). As a Bible teacher, I believe that no one except God had a greater effect on man's ancient history than the Jewish patriarchs. They were even greater than Alexander or Caesar.

As we explore Genesis 12:1–5, we read about the calling of Abraham. His father, Terah, moved their family group from the city of Ur in southern Mesopotamia to Haran, or Paddan Aram, in the north. God told Abraham (Abram) to leave the safety and comfort of his father's house in Haran (which is in northern Mesopotamia) and the city of Ur to travel to the land of Canaan and dwell there. He was chosen to have a special relationship with God, so he had to separate himself now from the gods of Mesopotamia. Abraham was chosen to be the father of God's chosen, special covenant people. According to history author H. L. Hester, "The calling of Abraham was the most important religious event since the fall of man." By faith, he obeyed God and traveled a long distance to a strange new land to establish a new life. This is never easy to do. He was then seventy-five years old. This was a test of faith. Abraham, his wife Sarah, his nephew Lot, and their immediate families moved to the land of Canaan (modern Israel). According to author and biblical chronology expert Jack Finegan, Abraham (Abram) entered Canaan in 1921 BC.

Because of famine, Abraham (Abram) and his family group traveled through Canaan, stopping briefly at Shechem and Bethel (Luz), then camped in Egypt before moving to Canaan. In Egypt, God blessed them with large flocks and herds. So soon after they arrived in the Holy Land, there was strife between Abraham's and Lot's herdsmen because the pasture land could not support them both. They separated, and Lot chose all the beautiful, well-watered, and prosperous plains of Jordan east toward the notably sinful city of Sodom (refer to Genesis 13).

In Genesis 14:4 and Genesis 14:18–19, we discover that Abraham became the hero in a war. His efforts helped liberate some local Canaanite cities from Mesopotamian control. He also freed his nephew Lot from captivity. As a result, Abraham met the mysterious Melchizedek, the king of Salem, and the priest of the Most High God. He blessed Abraham for his victory. Hebrews 7:1–3 and Psalm 110 provide more insight as to who Melchizedek was.

The meaning of his name is "my king is righteous." He was without parents. He had no beginning of days or end of life. He was made like the Son of God. Some Jewish rabbis have taught the legend that Melchizedek was actually Shem, the son of Noah. They believe that "no beginning of days" refers to the fact that due to the long life spans, he was the only person alive who was born before the flood.

Also they believe that "no end of life" refers to the fact that he was the oldest person alive on earth and that his contemporaries thought he would live forever. This may explain his lineage problem. The most important aspect of Melchizedek is his priesthood when compared to that of the Son of God, Lord Jesus. The Lord Jesus has a continual, or never-ending, ministry as God's great High Priest. It is interesting that Melchizedek gave Abraham bread and wine, which may be considered a preview of the Passover Seder, or the Lord's Supper by the Christians. Modern Jewish scholarship, however, discounts this view because traditionally, bread was symbolic of blessing, and wine was an agent to make food special. The name Melchizedek may have been a title used by Shem in the same fashion that the title Pharaoh is used to describe the kings of Egypt. His ancient city of Salem is modern Jerusalem, God's holy city (Zion).

In Genesis 15, we find the vitally important account of the Abrahamic covenant. The Messiah would descend through Abraham (Abram) through his children. Abraham's wife, Sarah (Sarai), was barren and unable to give him children. Abraham trusted God and entered into a suzerain covenant with Him. God promised that Abraham's descendants would be so numerous that it would be difficult to count them. God promised that Abraham's descendants would inherit the land of Canaan. Abraham was chosen to be the father of God's covenant people, who would carry out God's salvation plan for all mankind. As a result of this honor, God stated that anyone who blessed Abraham and his descendants would be blessed, but anyone who cursed them would be cursed (Read Genesis 12). Remember that throughout history, every nation that became an enemy of the Jewish people also became an enemy of God! A suzerain covenant is an agreement between a lord and a vassal. The lord provides protection, and the vassal provides obedience. Normally, during such an agreement, both parties entering the covenant will make promises to each other. However, in this case, God made all the promises. All Abraham was required to do was believe (Romans 4:2–3, Galatians 3:6–7). Our country must always be ready to support the nation of Israel to prosper and avoid God's judgment (Zechariah 12:9, Joshua

21:43). : the celebration of Purim is an excellent example of God's promise to Abraham (the book of Ester).

God took a long time to fulfill his promises of a son to Abraham, so he decided to take matters into his own hands and do something himself to bring about God's promised blessings. He had relations with his wife Sarah's handmaiden, Hagar, and had a child, Ishmael, through her. Abraham (Abram) and Sarah (Sarai) were raised in the city of Ur, where, according to Bible expert and author Rev. J. McGee, this was a common practice. However, this act was still a sin, and God did not approve of it. Ishmael is credited with being the father of the Arabs. About thirteen or fourteen years later, the patriarch Isaac, the son of promise, was born to Abraham's wife, Sarah. He was a miracle child because Sarah was ninety years old. The lineage of the Lord Jesus is traced from Isaac. Ishmael and his mother, Hagar, were sent away so that Isaac could inherit the blessings of God, according to the promises. God always keeps His promises. In our time and throughout history, the Jews and the Arabs have been mortal enemies, and in the twenty-first century, both people groups who descended from Abraham, both the Jews and Arabs, are in a heated dispute over the occupation of the promised land. Only the Messiah, Lord Jesus, can bring them lasting peace. Ishmael means "God will hear." The land belongs to the Jews.

In Genesis 17, we read about the covenant of circumcision. God renewed His covenant with Abraham (Abram). God changed his name from Abram to Abraham. Abram means "exalted father." Abraham means "father of a multitude." God gave him the sign of circumcision to identify his family and his descendants (future generations) as God's chosen people. The Messiah, Lord Jesus, repealed the rite of circumcision because all Gentiles who are redeemed through Him are now also His people. So we all now have a new covenant in His blood (Acts 10). God commanded that the circumcision must be performed on the eighth day after birth. Modern medicine has discovered that both vitamin K and prothrombin reach their efficiency on the eighth day, making it the perfect time to perform a circumcision. Abraham was then ninety-nine years old. Every male in his settlement or camp was circumcised.

As we continue to explore Genesis, we come to Genesis 18 and Genesis 19, where we read about righteous Lot and the wicked cities of Sodom and Gomorrah. We also discover the reason God destroyed these cities. I must stress that as a Bible history teacher, author, and scholar, I find that most authors agree it is rather difficult to write about this rather serious and very controversial subject, never to be avoided because the truth must be told regardless of the repercussions. In Genesis 18:24, the Lord and two angels visited Abraham. The Lord confirmed His promises to Abraham concerning a son, Isaac, who would be born soon after the visit. The Lord also informed Abraham of the coming judgment of Sodom and Gomorrah. Abraham pleaded with the Lord to save the city of Sodom if only ten righteous people were found. The Lord agreed. God is merciful. I believe that this is a theophany or appearance of the Lord Jesus in the Old Testament scriptures (John 8:56–58). It's possible that Lot's immediate family in Sodom were ten people. The two angels entered the city of Sodom, and righteous Lot, the nephew of Abraham, invited them into his house to spend the night in safety. But before it was time to lie down, a large number of raging homosexuals surrounded Lot's house and demanded that Lot send out the angels so that they could "know them," or rape them. The term "know them" is a reference to sexual contact (intercourse). For example, in Genesis 4:1, we read that Adam knew Eve sexually. The angels blinded the homosexuals and removed Lot and his family from Sodom. Then the Lord rained fire and brimstone (sulfur) upon the cities as a judgment for sin. This judgment is God's warning to all future generations. God loves sinners but hates sin—in this case, specifically the sin of homosexuality (see Leviticus 20:13 and Deuteronomy 23:17). Homosexuality is a perverse and very dangerous forbidden practice (see Jude 7, 2 Timothy 3, and Romans 1:26–27). Remember that this sin is so serious that God destroyed entire cities because of it.

Many teachers and students may be shocked or surprised to read this sobering truth. In the twenty-first century, homosexuality is often viewed as a human rights issue rather than as a moral or sin issue. It has been sold and widely accepted as an alternative lifestyle that is growing in popularity. But what is popular is not always right, and what is right is not always popular. Homosexuality is not a life-style, orientation, or civil or human rights issue. It is a very serious morals issue, and it is morally wrong! Nothing can ever change that. Our just and holy God demonstrated His divine wisdom, love, and great mercy toward the rest of mankind when He destroyed the evil, sinful cities of Sodom and Gomorrah. In doing so, our righteous God prevented the fear, sin, diseases, and depravity of homosexuality from spreading to other parts of the ancient world. There is nothing gay about it. This evil had to be purged!

The following true information is worth your sincere consideration because the modern professors are not allowed to teach you these facts. According to the FRI (Family Research Institute) in Colorado, USA, the average lifespan of male homosexuals is only thirty-nine years. This is the result of sexually transmitted diseases and suicides (Proverbs 14:34). Also, the FRI revealed that the top six American serial killers were practicing homosexuals. The modern term *sodomy* refers to the sinful, twisted, evil practices of Sodom.

In this new age of acceptance and tolerance, we who are teachers and students must search our conscience and take a stand for righteousness! Martin Luther King Jr. said, "Cowardice asks the question, is it safe? Experience asks the question, is it politic? Vanity asks the question, is it popular? Conscience asks the question is it right? And there is a time when one must take a position that is neither safe, nor politic, nor popular, but he must take it because his conscience tells him it is right." Remember that God never tolerates man's sin. However, the busy world around us is constantly fighting for the freedom to commit sins instead of God's true freedom from all sin through Jesus Christ, the Messiah. There is no pride in sin. Please don't hate them, always pray for them. but make a stand for the truth.

Genesis 19:3 is fascinating to those students who enjoy Bible trivia. This is the first time unleavened bread or matzo is recorded in Scripture. Matzo is traditionally known as the bread of affliction (suffering) (Kings 22:27). In the four Gospels, during the Last Supper, the Messiah, Lord Jesus, used matzo, or unleavened bread, to represent His battered body sacrificed for our sins on the cross, the Lord Jesus is the Passover Afikoman (Tzafun). Matzo represents sinlessness. Leaven is often used as a symbol for sin. Lot was free from the sins (leaven) of ancient Sodom. (1 Cor. 5:8)

In Genesis 19:26, Lot's wife looked back at Sodom (Mathew 26:22, Luke 22:19) as it was being destroyed and was turned into a pillar of salt. It is generally believed that just like the stubborn people of Sodom, she desired her sin more than God's salvation. Never look back at or desire sin. Never look to our past, only our future with Christ. We do not know why Lot's wife was turned into a pillar of salt except for the sin of disobedience, which we are all guilty of committing (Romans 3:23), but we can imagine just how much she missed her life in the city. It was said that her body walked out of the city but that she left her heart there (Mathew 6:19–22, Luke 18:32–33). The effect of an immoral, perverse, and addictive environment showed up in the lewd behavior patterns of Lot's daughters. They both committed incest with their father, Lot, when he was deliberately made drunk and had no control over it. The nations of Moab and Ammon are Lot's descendants (refer to Genesis 19:30–36). Throughout the Holy Bible, all sexual perversion was abhorred by God, so my readers should avoid all forms of sexual immorality. Your physical and spiritual health depends on it. A virtuous life is a blessed life! The choice is up to you. If you love God, repent and obey Him.

The exact location of the ruins of the evil cities of Sodom and Gomorrah has puzzled Bible scholars and historians for centuries. However, this mystery may be solved. The dominant theory accepted by many scholars places them under the southern waters of the Dead Sea, where ancient ruins and large sulfur (brimstone) deposits have been found (John 3:16).

Now we come to one of the most exciting parts of Scripture. In Genesis 22, known as the Akeda, we learn that God tested Abraham. This was to prove just how much Abraham really loved and trusted God. If you want to be a holy and godly person, expect to be tested. God told Abraham to sacrifice his son Isaac as a burnt offering. This was the son of promise and blessing and the continuation of the Messianic line. It is believed by many theologians that by this time, Isaac was probably a teenager. I agree with their opinion. I believe he was probably a teenager. However, the famous Bible commentator J. V. McGee believes Isaac was about thirty to thirty-three years old, which is the same age the Lord Jesus was when He became God's sacrifice for our sin. An old Jewish legend states that Isaac was thirty-seven years old when he became the faith-testing sacrifice. That same year, Sarah, his mother, died. Only God knows the truth concerning this fact (2 Corinthians 5:21). Note that because of the longer life spans at that time, Isaac might have matured at an older age. Older may have been younger then.

Abraham must have felt deep and great emotional trauma and remorse. Yet he obeyed God. To please God, we must give Him our best. Abraham was willing to do this regardless of his suffering and pain. Do not underestimate the results of sin and the price of salvation. I have learned that if you truly love someone, you will love until it hurts. Abraham truly loved God and proved it.

Isn't it amazing that Isaac did not run away when he discovered that he was the sacrifice? He trusted and obeyed his father even unto death, just as the Lord Jesus did (see Job 13:15). It is a shame that many young people do not follow Isaac's example. In the beginning of the twenty-first century, the sins of rebellion and disobedience are common practices among the youth, teenagers, and also the young adults of our society. They do not honor and respect their elders (Exodus 12:17, Mark 7:10). It seems that most of them have no knowledge of sin or faith in God (Matthew 18:2–4). Sadly, according to Rev. B. Gothert and other experts, modern statistics have proven that the next generation will sin worse than their parents did (Titus 2:13). Isaac made Sarah laugh. The name Isaac means "one laughs." Bible teacher and author V. R. Benson stated that "Isaac is a type of the Lord Jesus. Both Isaac and Jesus had been offered up as a sacrifice." Both obeyed their father.

God was convinced that Abraham was willing to sacrifice his son to prove he loved and trusted God. As a result, God provided a ram for the burnt offering and stopped Abraham from killing Isaac. The ram, or lamb, is symbolic of the Messiah, the Lord Jesus, God's substitute (John 1:29). The test of obedience and faith of Abraham sacrificing his son is a prototype of God can be offering His only Son, the Lord Jesus, found in the four Gospels. God gave us His very best. Mt. Moriah, was where Abraham was tested by God, but theologians can possibly believe it is the present site of the Temple Mount in Jerusalem or the site of the crucifixion or Adam's Grave; but I don't know. (read 2 Chronicles 3).

In Genesis 24, we read about the arranged marriage of Isaac and Rebecca. Abraham did not want his son to marry a woman from the sinful, ungodly people of Canaan, so he sent his servant (who was Eliezer) to find a wife for Isaac among his own people in the city of Nahor, or Haran, in Paddan Aram. Unlike our rebellious young people today, Isaac gladly obeyed his father and accepted a wife wisely chosen for him by others; and Rebecca demonstrated great faith, accepting Isaac as her husband without seeing him first. Old Testament scholar Dr. Leon Wood believes Isaac and Rebecca were married in 2026 BC. Please refer to the timeline for the Old Testament by Dr. Riss. Some Orthodox Jewish people still have arranged marriages today (Hebrews 11:1). Isaac was forty years old then.

In some modern Bible colleges across America, it is generally believed that after Isaac and Rebecca were married, it took twenty years to have children. This was because Rebecca was barren. Isaac was sixty years old when the twins, Esau and Jacob, were born. God's time is always the best time to have children. According to author Stephen Miller, Sarah died at the great old age of 127, when Isaac was just 37 years old. After the death of Sarah, Abraham remarried, had other children, and lived to be 175 years old. Note that Father Abraham has millions of spiritual children. They are the brave men and women throughout out human history who have demonstrated great faith. They accepted the Messiah, the Lord Jesus, and often suffered or died for their faith. They are his true and everlasting heritage (Galatians 1:7). Isaac was God's chosen servant and honored to continue the vital lineage of the Messiah and receive God's special blessings, but poor Ishmael was not chosen. However, for Abraham's sake, God also blessed Ishmael with wives and land. He and Isaac both made peace and buried their father, Abraham, in Hebron. Ishmael became an archer and dwelt in the land of Paran. His descendants settled in Arabia and live there today.

Many modern history books may tell you that the ancient Philistines were a sea people who landed in Canaan (Israel) in about 1175 BC or later, well after the time of the patriarchs. Evolutionists rewrite history to support their sensational and convoluted but often-believed agenda. However, in Genesis 26, Isaac strived with the Philistines over water rights. So the Philistines were well established in the Holy Land before the time of the patriarchs, about 2166 BC. Modern Palestine is probably named after the Philistines.

In the book of Genesis, chapter 26, God appeared to Isaac and renewed the Abrahamic covenant with him. During a famine, Isaac lived in the land of the Philistines. He pretended his wife, Rebecca, was his sister so the Philistines would not kill him and marry her. Earlier in Genesis, Abraham did the same thing in Egypt quite possibly during the reign of Pharaoh Yotef II. We have a very strong tendency to act like our fathers. Just ask any psychiatrist (read Genesis 12:12).

Genesis does not discuss very much about the life of Isaac, so we will now move on to his descendants. The twin sons of Isaac are Jacob and Esau. The name Esau means "ruddy" (or red) or "hairy," and the name Jacob means "heel grabber or supplanter." They are first mentioned in Genesis 25–27. When they were born, Jacob grabbed Esau's heel. Some students may see an enlightening historical parallel between Jacob and Esau and Adam's sons, Cain and Abel. In both instances, one brother is chosen and accepted by God, and the other is rejected for moral reasons (Genesis 4:4–5, Romans 9:13, Amis 1:56). In history, Esau's descendants, the Edomites, were for the most part subservient to Israel but often revolted. However, in respect to Jacob, Messianic rabbi M. Baleston of Messengers of the New Covenant in New Jersey believes that the word *supplanter* is an incorrect definition that is historically used by anti-Semites to denigrate the character of Jewish people. I tend to agree with him, but I also believe that some of the authors that used the word *supplanter* were certainly not anti-Semitic but loved the Jewish people like I do. (Throughout recorded history, Jacob's descendants, the Jewish people, have been a tremendous blessing to all the nations of the world; their great accomplishments are unparalleled Lord Jesus is Jewish.)

We discover in Genesis 25:24–34 that Jacob purchased the birthright from Esau. The birthright was not important to Esau, so when he was hungry, he sold it to Jacob for a pot of beans or hot soup. The birthright allowed the oldest son to inherit his father's goods and property. Now it was necessary to get Isaac to approve the transaction. So Jacob listened to his mother and deceived his father into blessing him (see Genesis 27). Isaac was blind, so cleverly, Jacob pretended to be Esau to be blessed because Isaac loved Esau and was preparing to bless him. This produced great animosity between Jacob and Esau. Jacob had to flee to Paddan Aram and visit his uncle Laban for a number of years to prevent Esau from harming him (Genesis 28:1–4, Hebrews 11:20). Esau begged his father, Isaac, to bless him, but only Jacob received the blessings.

On his way to Haran, or Paddan Aram, or Naharaim, Jacob camped near Bethel (Luz). He had a vision in a dream of a ladder reaching heaven. In the dream, God renewed the Abrahamic covenant with Jacob. He was now endowed with the promises that God had made to Abraham. Jacob was afraid and established a pillar as a monument in that place (Genesis 28:12–16). In those days, monuments were built to remind the future generations that an important event took place in that location, "the Lord Jesus is our ladder to Heaven" (John 14:6). Jacob vowed to give or tithe 10 percent of his wealth to God, providing he was blessed. According to renowned Messianic rabbi M. Baleston, the law of Moses which came approximately six hundred years later, required all Jewish males to title 23 percent of their wealth to God, not 10 percent. I support modern biblical tithing. God must be our first priority! Always give. Be generous.

Shortly after Jacob arrived in Paddan Aram, he fell in love with his cousin Rachel, the daughter of Laban. Jacob agreed to work for seven years for her hand in marriage. However, his uncle Laban deceived him and gave him his daughter Leah instead, hoping to get him to work another seven years. The custom was that the older daughter was to be married first. Jacob then agreed to work an additional seven years for Rachel. To achieve anything, we must have faith and work hard for it (Genesis 29:18–31). Uncle Laban succeeded in cheating the rather experienced cheater, it looks like. Jacob never suspected he was duped.

As we study Genesis 29:25 to Genesis 31:13, we discover that Jacob and Laban treated each other with deceit and underhanded trickery. It looks like they cheated each other apparently whenever possible. For example, Jacob outwitted Laban with his livestock breeding, and Laban changed Jacob's wages ten times. They were both crafty businessmen, but the major difference is that Jacob received the blessing of God. According to Jewish scholarship, Laban means "white or like milk."

In Paddan Aram, Jacob had eleven sons (see Genesis 29:29–30:24). Their names are Reuben, Simeon, Levi, Judah, Dan, Naphtali, Gad, Asher, Issachar, Zebulon, and Joseph. Jacob's twelfth son, Benjamin, was born after Jacob left Haran, or Paddan Aram. He also had a daughter named Dinah. From these twelve sons of Jacob came the twelve tribes of Israel, the Jewish people—God's covenant people.

Jacob worked for Laban for perhaps fourteen to twenty years, maybe more. Then Jacob sensed the growing hostility of his uncle Laban and Laban's sons toward his family because of their prosperity. God also told him to return home (Genesis 31:3). So he and his wives had a family meeting, and then they decided it was time to go. It is believed that Uncle Laban had no intention of letting Jacob and his family leave. Laban was blessed as a result of God blessing Jacob. So to prevent Laban from stopping them, they left without telling him. Laban soon followed after them, and his men overtook them at Mizpah. God warned Laban not to harm Jacob. Here, Jacob and Laban negotiated a contract, or peace treaty; and then they both departed each to their own country. Jacob sent gifts ahead to make peace with Esau (Genesis 31:1–55).

You may be wondering what happened to Esau during the years that Jacob was in Paddan Aram. It appears that he was forgiven and also blessed by God. As we read on, Genesis 33 and 36 show that Esau became a powerful man in the land of Seir. His new name was Edom, and the Edomites are his descendants. When they finally met,

Jacob bowed down to Esau seven times either to show respect for his high position or perhaps out of fear, to save his life. Esau and Jacob made peace with each other, and Esau hugged Jacob. Esau wanted to accompany Jacob to keep him safe. All hatred was gone. All sin was forgiven. God can patch up any relationship. Edom means "from red to red" or "very red."

Genesis 32:24–32 is an amazing piece of Scripture. Along the way to meet Esau, Jacob wrestled with a man or an angel in the form of a man. They wrestled from night until morning. Jacob would not let go until he was blessed. The man or angel told Jacob that his name was now Israel because he had power with God and man and prevailed. Israel means "prince of God." This may possibly be a theophany or appearance by the Lord Jesus in the Old Testament. The Lord Jesus is the incarnation, having two natures—both God and man.

Genesis 34 records that Jacob's daughter Dinah was defiled, or raped, by Shechem, who was prince of the city of Shechem (near Shalem), which Jacob was camped next to. The city was perhaps named after the prince himself or a distant ancestor. But after this sinful act, Jacob agreed to their marriage, providing all the males in the city were circumcised, leaving them helpless and in pain. As a result, Jacob's sons Simeon and Levi took revenge on Prince Shechem, slaughtered all the males, and pillaged the city. Jacob and his family left immediately, and they traveled to Bethel (Luz), where God appeared to Jacob (Israel). God told them to go there as a call to repentance, holiness, and freedom from sin (please see Genesis 35:2). Bethel is where they felt safe (Psalm 91, 27; Genesis 28). Today, our country needs a serious call to repentance. Sin is everywhere.

In order to fully understand the meaning of the book of Genesis, the serious student should have a working knowledge of Messianic prophecy. Genesis 38 is so important because it established the lineage of the Messiah. Judah was Jacob's son of promise (Genesis 49:10). The Messiah would descend through Judah through his children. Judah's first two sons died early in life as a result of sin and a fallen human nature. God slew them. He promised the widow of both of his sons, Tamar, that she would be married to his third son,

Shelah, when he came of age. But Judah did not keep his promise to Tamar. So she deceived him by playing the harlot with him. She then cleverly exposed his folly, and he admitted his guilt (sin) (Genesis 38:24–26). They had two male children, twins; and thus, the Messianic line continued onward through the centuries until the Lord Jesus was born. The term *Jewish* comes from *Judah*. For more information on the subject, read *Messianic Prophecy of the Old Testament* by Kligerman. The account of Judah and Tamar makes for a real-life soap opera! *Judah* means "praise." Jesus Christ is the lion of the tribe of Judah (Revelations 4:5).

The most famous son of Jacob was Joseph. He was used mightily by God. Joseph was the firstborn son of Rachel, whom he loved, and Joseph was the son of Jacob's old age. So Jacob (Israel) treated him with favoritism. This was demonstrated by Joseph having received a coat of many colors from his father (refer to Genesis 37:3–4). We don't have enough data concerning the purpose of the coat. Perhaps many colors may refer to the rainbow, representing God's everlasting covenant with mankind after the deluge (refer to chapter 3). This extraordinary coat may have been a symbol of rank or power. Jacob may have intended Joseph to be the future leader of the family. As a result of the favoritism, Joseph's brothers were very envious of him. Jacob (Israel) showed preference to Joseph as well by assigning him the task of inspecting the work of his brothers. God prepared Joseph to be a leader.

Joseph knew that God had a special purpose in mind for him. In one of his dreams, the sun, moon, and stars (referring to Jacob, Leah, and his brothers) bowed down to him. This dream also refers to the nation of Israel (refer to Revelation 12:1). This really upset his brothers. One day, when Joseph went to inspect his brothers' work, they captured him and planned to kill him to stop the fulfillment of his dreams. They then decided, however, to fake his death; and they sold him to the Ishmaelites (Arabs), who were traveling to Egypt (see Genesis 37:12–36). Jacob (Israel) was very sad upon hearing this false report of his son's death.

Joseph was sold for twenty pieces of silver, the price for a servant or slave, then went on to be a savior to his family (see Genesis

37:27–29). The Lord Jesus was sold for thirty pieces of silver, the price paid for God's suffering servant, and he became the Savior of the world (see Matthew 27:3–5, Jer. 11, 12). Joseph can be a preview or forerunner of the Messiah, Lord Jesus, or an example of Christ. The Bible has many examples of lives that parallel Christ such as Elisha (2 Kings 1:13). According to radio commentator J. V. McGee, "There is no one in Scripture who is more like Christ in his person and experiences than Joseph." Joseph means "to increase or may God add."

The Ishmaelites either traveled with or sold Joseph to their Arab cousins the Midianites, from Arabia, who are believed to possible be his cousins descended from Abraham through his second wife, Keturah. In Egypt, the Midianites or Ishmaelites then sold Joseph to Potiphar, an officer of Pharaoh. Joseph proved to be so trustworthy that Potiphar gave him authority over the affairs of his household. God blessed Potiphar's house for Joseph's sake so that everything he touched became prosperous (Genesis 39:6). But based on the false accusations of Potiphar's wife, whose sexual advances Joseph had wisely rejected, he was unjustly sent to prison. Through many trials, Joseph never lost his faith in God (Romans 13). In those days, wives were considered a symbol or sign of status. Many high officials were eunuchs, and Potiphar might have been an eunuch and thus unable to satisfy his wife. This is only an assumption, but we can only guess at her sinful motives concerning Joseph. We do know, however, that he was personally tempted, rejected her overtures, and remained pure before God (Genesis 39).

All this was done according to God's plan (Romans 8:28). It can be an adventure when we follow God's plan for our lives. So let God use you for His glory. God used Joseph in prison. Pharaoh's chief butler and his chief baker were imprisoned for offending the king. Maybe they tried to poison him. Through God's help, Joseph interpreted their dreams, and his explanations came true. The butler was forgiven, and the baker was executed (Genesis 40:5–23). This blessing from God would soon get him released from prison.

About two years later, Pharaoh had a dream that upset him. No one in his court, however, could explain them to Pharaoh. Then the chief butler remembered Joseph and his ability to interpret dreams. With God's help, Joseph interpreted Pharaoh's dream concerning a devastating famine seven years into the future. Pharaoh promoted Joseph to second in command of Egypt, placing him personally in charge of storing away food for the time of the famine (Genesis 41). Joseph was given an Egyptian name, Zaphnath-Paaneah, which means "food man" and "gives life" or "revealer," depending upon the translator.

Upon exploring the book of Genesis, students and teachers must consider the information in this paragraph very, very seriously. This is an excellent example of man's faith in God. In fact, this is the type of faith God's people should all have! Joseph had to be tried and tested before God could use him. Those who desire to be holy and sincerely love our holy, righteous God must suffer. Remember that a life of ease and comfort accomplishes nothing beneficial and tends to corrupt our character (Ephesians 5:1). It is generally believed that Joseph was only seventeen years old when he was sold into slavery, and he was thirty years old when he became second in command in Egypt. So it is believed he was in prison for approximately twelve or thirteen years—or according to some scholars, four or five years (we are not certain just how long or how old he was). Yet during all that time, Joseph did not lose his faith. He truly suffered for many years when any hope seemed impossible, but he continued to fully trust God for his salvation. When you find yourself in impossible situations, remember Joseph and trust in God for your salvation. All my readers must learn from this example. Our survival often depends on recognizing God's purpose in every negative experience! Tough trials can strengthen character and prepare us for success. It was said that "through all his trials, Joseph was being conformed into the image of Christ" (please refer to Psalm 2:12 and Hebrews 11).

Many teachers and students may be interested in just who the Pharaoh was during the time that Joseph was in Egypt. The subject can create divisions among scholars because there are many strong opinions. H. H. Halley believes that Joseph was in Egypt during the sixteenth dynasty, but as a long-time student or scholar of history, I can find no significant evidence to support this belief except for a famine. But there are many famines recorded in Ancient Egyptian history. Some of the scholars who support a late exodus date for the patriarchs place Joseph in history around 1786 BC to 1570 BC, between dynasties, during the reign of the Hyksos kings. But there is no tangible evidence to support this view. According to Professors Hill and Walton and Dr. Collins, Joseph lived from 1915 BC to about 1805 BC. Thus, he lived during the reign of Sesostris II. King Sesostris (Senusret) II reigned from about 1897 BC or 1888 BC to 1878 BC, during the Middle Kingdom and the twelfth dynasty. However, it is sometimes difficult to have precise dating of the reigns of the pharaohs of Egypt. This is primarily because of the possible practice of coregency. Dr. R. Riss of Pillar Christian College in New Jersey teaches that Joseph arrived in Egypt in 1898 BC just before Sesostris (Senusret) II began to reign. In Genesis 45:8, Joseph tells his family that he is a father to Pharaoh. This suggests that that Sesostris was young when he became king and that his father, Ammenemes II, may have been the pharaoh when Joseph was in prison. Basing my research on dates provided by Hill and Walton, Joseph died in 1805 BC. This also places him well within the time of the twelfth dynasty of Egyptian kings. This would probably be about eighty years after he became second in command in Egypt, so he would have also lived during the reigns of Sesostris III and his son, Amenemhet III. During the reign of Amenemhet (Ammenemes) from 1842 BC to 1797 BC, a canal was built in Egypt called Bahr Yusuf, or Joseph's Canal. What better proof can we then have as to whom the Pharaohs were during the time of Joseph?

As we study Genesis 42–46, we discover that during the famine, Joseph's brothers, who sold him into slavery, were hungry. The famine was also in the Holy Land. They needed food, so they came to Egypt to buy grain. They had to deal directly with Joseph, but they did not recognize him. Joseph's earlier dreams about his brothers bowing down to him were fulfilled when they came to Egypt to buy food. After accusing them of spying and testing their character in many ways to see if they repented, Joseph told them who he was. He forgave them for the wrong they did to him. What they did for evil, God used for good to protect them (Genesis 50:20). We must always forgive others so that God can use us for His glory (Matthew 18:21–22). All that happened was according to God's plan.

Upon hearing that Joseph was alive, Jacob and his entire family moved into Egypt. This was seventy or seventy-five people. At that time, Sesostris (Senusret) II died, and Sesostris III began to reign from about 1878 BC to 1843 BC. Remember that because of possibly coregencies, it is difficult to be accurate when dating the pharaohs. Jacob adopted Joseph's two sons, Manasseh and Ephraim, making them equal with his own sons (Genesis 46–48). Their names are listed as two of the twelve tribes of Israel (refer to Exodus). *Manasseh* means "to forget the past," and *Ephraim* means "a fruitful present life," reflecting on Joseph's past and present lives. It is now worth mentioning that the descendants of Joseph's son Ephraim are often referred to in the books of Joshua, Judges, and 1 and 2 Samuel as having had a major role in Hebrew history.

God used Joseph to prepare a place in Egypt to preserve His people, Israel, during the famine. Then later in history, God allowed His people to become slaves in Egypt for 430 years to prepare them for nationhood, the Exodus, the Ten Commandments, the Holy Profits, and the Messiah. They will always be God's chosen people (Jeremiah 31–32, Romans 11).

In Genesis 50, we read the account of the deaths of Jacob and Joseph. Before he died, Jacob gathered his family together and blessed them. The blessings of Jacob (Israel) were prophecies that were later in history fulfilled when the Jewish people returned to the promised land of Canaan (modern-day Israel). Blessings were a testimony, allowed security, passed on inheritance, and were used to prophesy the future. They always had a serious impact on the recipient (read Joshua, Judges, and Samuel). May God's Holy Bible become a powerful blessing to you, and may this book also bless you. Jacob (Israel) died at the age of 147 years and was buried in Hebron, in the land of Canaan, in a manner similar to that of a great person or king. Joseph died at the age of 110. He might have lived during the reigns of four pharaohs. Ancient Egyptian records indicate that 110 years was considered to be the ideal life span. Maybe Joseph had something to do with that belief. It's worth consideration. When he died, Joseph was embalmed in the Egyptian style and placed in a coffin or sarcophagus. About four hundred years later, his body was taken back to Canaan during the Exodus and buried in Shechem (Josh. 24:32). However, it may be speculated that some modern-day liberal historians may quite possibly believe he was buried again later in history with his fathers, possibly in the field of Machpelah in Hebron, but Holy Scripture is clear that he was buried in Shechem or in Sychar, near Shechem (John 4:5). The city of Hebron (Kirjath-Arba), is the ancient burial site of the patriarchs and their wives. So Hebron is highly honored as a Jewish holy place.

I believe that if our rebellious youth living today will use the patriarchs as role models, then God will bless our nation. The patriarchs' lives are an example for us to follow, and the patriarchs lived for and obeyed God. If only people would live like that today, we all would be blessed and safe. So study the Holy Bible and learn to live well.

With the death of Joseph in chapter 50, the exciting book of Genesis comes to an end. But God's wonderful salvation plan and the exciting history of the nation of Israel and the Messiah continues onward throughout the sixty-six books of the Bible. There is no doubt that all of mankind's history depends upon them. I hope you enjoy reading the Holy Bible as much as I do. It's always a rewarding adventure. May God always bless you in your research and studies. No matter what book of the Bible you study or what period in history you are interested in, remember that all the time, God is good and that His love is everlasting mercy for all.

STUDENT'S NOTES

ARCHAEOLOGY AND THE BOOK OF GENESIS

CHAPTER 7

Archaeology and the Book of Genesis

QUITE OFTEN, EVIDENCE is necessary to prove that something is true. Ancient history and the Genesis account are no exception to this rule. Over the centuries since creation, much of our history has been lost or rewritten to support the hypothesis of evolution. Busy students will usually accept whatever they are taught (such as dangerous neo-Darwinism) without questioning it to receive good grades. So in the busy world around us, students seldom take the time to search for the truth. However, there is always overwhelming natural, historical, and ancient archeological evidence supporting the book of Genesis. It has been said that archaeology is defined as "the mirror of the ages," reflecting our history. In the previous six chapters of this book, I have presented many examples of scientific and historical evidence. So in this brief but informative chapter, I will deal with some of the better-known archaeological discoveries now available to the public as of the year AD 2022 or 2023, when the first edition of this book will be published. Remember that there are many ancient artifacts (OOPArts) that do not support today's popular uniformitarian evolutionary assumption, so they are hidden from the general public. According to the renowned antiquities expert C. Berlitz, "It has been calculated that less than 10% of the records of antiquity have come down to us." So there is only a small percentage of artifacts to examine. Therefore, many mysteries still exist concerning our past history and the book of Genesis. My research, however, has been rewarding.

I personally believe that all sixty-six books of the Bible can be supported by many amazing and trustworthy archaeological discoveries, thus giving credibility to the Bible as a whole. Genesis has the most significant need for tangible support because it deals with man's origins. Since its conception to the present date, evolution has been sadly based upon false assumptions, deprived of any real evidence to support its sensational uniformitarian claims. The book of Genesis and special creation, however, are strongly supported by a great deal of evidence founded upon truth. God doesn't monkey around (refer to chapters 1 and 3)!

Because I intended to keep this book as brief as possible, I will now present a list of fourteen archaeological discoveries that give tangible, credible support to the wonderful Genesis account. I challenge the diligent student to research further than I did and produce even more information. But for now, let's examine the exciting discoveries listed below.

1. *The Weld-Blundell Prism.* This is an artifact from the year 2170 BC or 1800 BC that was recorded by scribe Nur Nin-Subur, giving us a fine historical lineage of the ancient world. The Weld-Blundell Prism provides data that gives credible support to the long life spans of people living before the deluge. It informs us that the first two kings in history reigned from the city of Eridu. This city is believed by many to be the site of the garden of Eden.

2. *The city of Babylon (Babel), Akkadian Babilu.* The mysterious Tower of Babel was constructed here. The possible sites are the Temple of Nebo and the cylinder of Borsippa. Another name for the Tower of Babel is Etemenanki, meaning "top reaches to heaven." Babel, or Babylon, is approximately fifty or sixty miles from Baghdad and is one of man's oldest cities. Babylon was the wonder city of the mysterious ancient world. The walls had 250 towers and one hundred gates of brass. There were ferry boats, bridges, and a tunnel under the Euphrates river

fifteen feet wide and twelve feet high. In modern times, attempts have been made to restore the city (Swaggart, *Study Bible*). New York is a modern day, Babylon.

3. *The Akkadian Rahasis tablets, or Atra-Hasis epic.* They are believed to be from the year 1625 BC. They provide us with the accounts of creation itself as well as population growth and also the deluge, or flood. They have many wonderful similarities to the biblical accounts of the world before mankind was created and also the Genesis record. The folk hero is Atrahasis.

4. *The Sumerian Gilgamesh epic.* This famous literary work from the date 2654, 2700, or 2000 BC (or could be older) has a deluge, or flood, story with amazing similarities to the Genesis account, complete with the ark, the birds, and the mountain as well as a remarkable description of Eden, with the serpent and tree of life. However, it does not emphasize the vitally important moral dimension found in the book of Genesis. Author Ian Wilson believes that Gilgamesh lived in Northern Mesopotamia, but the epic was written in the south. The Sumerian name for Noah is Utnapishtim. Gilgamesh is portrayed as an evil tyrant, and he could possibly be Nimrod. The evidence suggests that Noah may have used a compass. I love compasses. Let the book of Genesis be your compass leading you to the Lord Jesus. No other direction matters.

5. *The Egyptian Memphite theology.* This work is dated at about the thirteenth century BC. It refers to creation as happening by God's spoken Word (ex nihilo) from nothing. Also, it says that God created the Sabbath and rested after the work of creation, similar to the wonderful Genesis account.

6. *The list of Sumerian kings.* Written in about the year 2100 BC, this account provides us with one of history's first mentions of the deluge. It divides the ancient Mesopotamian

kings into two groups: one before the flood and one after the flood of Noah. The kings before the deluge had very long names and very long lives.

7. *The ancient city of Ur.* This ancestral home of Abraham and Sarah was discovered in modern Iraq (Mesopotamia). It might have been founded as far back as 2500 BC but may be older and began to decline and fall possibly during the lifetime of the patriarchs. Ur was a center of pagan religions. This city has one of the first libraries of ancient times.

8. *The city of Eridu, or Abu Shahrain.* The ruins of Eridu were originally discovered by explorers Halls and Thompson of the British Museum. It is about twelve miles south of ancient Ur. It is believed by many teachers, historians, and Bible scholars to be located on the site of the garden of Eden. It is one of man's oldest cities, probably built shortly after the deluge.

9. *The city of Haran, or Paddan Aram, or Naharaim.* This important Jewish holy place and ancestral home of the patriarchs was built or founded in the second millennium BC. It continues to exist today in Eastern Turkey. Also found near Haran are the villages of Serug and Nahor, which still have the names of Abraham's ancestors. It is tangible proof that the patriarchs existed. *Paddan Aram* means "plain of Aram." *Naharaim* means "the two rivers."

10. *The Beni Hasan painting.* This fine work of art has been dated 1900 BC. It shows a caravan of hematic or Semitic people from Canaan (Israel) traveling to Egypt to conduct business just like Joseph's brothers in Genesis during the famine. It shows us how people looked and lived during the time of the patriarchs.

11. *The city of Nimrud (Nimrod).* This is a remarkable ruin located just southwest of modern Baghdad in Iraq. The name of the ancient city is tangible evidence and therefore

gives us a vivid testimony to the existence of the powerful world leader and mighty hunter king Nimrod, the evil, tyrannical son of Cush, recorded in Genesis (see chapter 4).

12. *The Dead Sea Scrolls.* This wonderful new discovery made in 1947 in a cave in Qumran, Israel, has provided us with a unique insight into the origins of the Bible. According to Eisenman and Wise, the Dead Sea Scrolls contain excerpts from the Holy Bible identical to Scripture available today (KJV).

13. *The four Gospels.* This portion of the New Testament, probably written in the first century from AD 48 to 95, presents us with the powerful testimony of the Messiah, Lord Jesus. His most authoritative references validate the book of Genesis. Please read Matthew 19:4–6, 24:37–39; Mark 10:4–9; Luke 11:49–51, 17:26-32; and John 7:21–23, 8:44 (KJV).

14. *The Grand Canyon, USA.* The Grand Canyon is too vast and wide to have been caused by the Colorado River. It is now believed that Noah's flood created it as it is 277 miles long and up to 18 miles wide, with a depth of over a mile (6,000 feet). Geology shows us that there is no other explanation. I hope to see it some day.

The archaeological evidence that I presented above is a powerful testimony to the validity of the book of Genesis. The absolute truth is out there. Most ancient and modern literary works do not have this kind of support. If I ever decide to expand on this book, then I am sure my list presented above will grow much longer. Remember that there are still many mysterious artifacts in museums all around the world that may someday present us with a more complete and sobering picture of our past history. Yet any serious student can appreciate my present research. The further we advance into the future, the more difficult is becomes to prove the events in our ancient and exciting past. But as time marches on and our moral and ethical values continue to change, the book of Genesis will always remain a wonderful part of our past, always affecting our present and our future. Whoever said evolution makes no sense (cents) is wrong. It makes millions of dollars, but it is still wrong. So powerful people can spend lots of money preventing archaeologists from discovering support for biblical truth and the media from exposing the false teachings of today, but the Lord Jesus said, "You shall know the truth and the truth shall set you free" (John 8:31–32).

STUDENT'S NOTES

TIME LINE

TIME LINE

Chronology of the Book of Genesis

Creation. Archbishop Ussher, 4004 BC; Dr. Chittick, around 4000 BC; H. Camping, about 11,013 BC; the Mayans, about 3104 or 3948 BC; Jack Finegan, 3760 BC; Ian Wilson, 4004 BC; H. H. Halley, around 4000 BC; the Septuagint, 5500 BC; Modern Jewish scholarship, 3760 BC; the Anglo-Saxons, 5200 BC; the Irish, based upon Bishop Usher's work, 4000 BC; and the Scots, 4000 BC.

The deluge, or flood, of Noah. Archbishop Ussher, 2348 BC; H. Camping 4990 BC; Rabbi Teitz of the Jewish Education Center in Elizabeth, New Jersey, 2100 or 3766 BC; Jack Finegan, 2104 BC; the Samaritan Pentateuch, about 3000 BC; the Septuagint, 3300 BC; R. Young, 2348 BC; Stephen Leston, 2300 BC; the Mayans, about 3135 BC; Anglo-Saxons, about 2247 BC; the Toltecs, 1,716 years after creation; Dr. Bruce Masse, 2807 BC; and Daniel S. Ward, 1,656 years after Adam was created.

The Tower of Babel. The time of Peleg, H. Camping, about 3153– 2914 BC; H. H. Halley, about 101 years after the flood; Rabbi Teitz of JEC, 2030 or 1996 BCE; R. Young, time of Peleg or 126 years after the flood, 2222 BC, and time of Nimrod's death, 2218 BC; B. Setterfield, time of Peleg, about 530 years after the flood; Dr. H. Morris of ICR, just before 3500 BC; the Catholic encyclopedia, about 870 years after the deluge; and renowned Professor Rash—after the death of Peleg.

Abraham. Archbishop Ussher, born 1996 BC; H. H. Halley, 2000 BC; Hill and Walton, 2166 BC to 1991 BC; Southwest Institute of Biblical and Theological Studies in New Mexico, based upon Galatians 3:15–19, dates 1951 BC to 1776 BC; *Jewish Time Line Encyclopedia*, 1813 BC to 1638 BC; Stephen Leston, 2166 BC; the Dealy Bible Study (Internet), was born about 2000 BC; Dr. Leon Wood, 2166 BC to 1991 BC; Dr. L. Richards, date of birth was 2125 BC; and H. L. Hester, 1900 BC.

Isaac. Hill and Walton, 2067 BC to 1886 BC; Southwest Institute of Biblical and Theological Studies, based upon Galatians 3:15–19, dates 1851 BC to 1671 BC; Dr. Leon Wood, married on 2026 BC; and Dr. L. Richards, date of birth was 2065 BC.

Jacob (Israel). Hill and Walton, 2003 BC to 1859 BC; Southwest Institute of Biblical and Theological Studies, based upon Galatians 3:15–19, dates 1791 BC to 1644 BC; H. Camping, born 2007 BC; *Jewish Time Line Encyclopedia*, 1653 BC to 1506 BC; Dr. Leon Wood, 2006 BC to 1959 BC; and Dr. L. Richards, date of birth was 2005 BC.

Joseph. Hill and Walton, 1915 BC to 1805 BC; H. Camping, date of Joseph's death was in 1806 BC; Rabbi Teitz, Jewish Education Center in Elizabeth, New Jersey, 1844 BC; Stephen Miller, about 1800 BC; Dr. R. Riss Joseph, entered Egypt in 1898 BC and the reign of Pharaoh Senusret in about 1878 BC; Dr. Leon Wood, 1915 BC to 1805; and Dr. L. Richards, date of birth was 1915 BC.

Note: All of the information in this brief chapter does not necessarily reflect my opinion as the author of this book. Most time lines, however, do not contain this much data; so students can form an accurate idea as to the proper dates and events, depending on which scholarship the students will trust. All the names quoted above are competent, well-recognized experts regarding the dating of events recorded in Genesis in biblical and ancient history. More precise dates may become available as new discoveries are found. I encourage students to research and discover more pertinent data. The information I have provided above will aid teachers, pastors, librarians, students, and scholars in their future research projects. May God bless you in all your efforts and assignments, and may His Holy Word live in your heart.

SELECTED BIBLIOGRAPHY

Bailey, James. *The God Kings & Titans*. New York City, New York, USA: St. Martin's Press, 2000.

Baxter's "A Walk though Genesis" (Internet). USA. https://bible.org/seriespage/1-walk-through-book-genesis.

Berlitz, Charles. *Mysteries from Forgotten Worlds*. Garden City, New York, USA: Doubleday Publishers, 1990.

Berlitz, Charles. *The Lost Ship of Noah*. New York City, USA: Putman and Sons, 1988.

Benson, V. R. *A Bible Study on Genesis*. New Paris, Indiana, USA: World Missionary Press, 1991.

Benton, W. *Britannica Atlas*. Rand McNally and Benton.

Brown, David. *Ape Man, Science or Myth?* Missouri, USA: Creations Science Assoc.

Camping, Harold. *Adam When?* California, USA: Family Radio.

Camping, Harold. *The Biblical Calendar of History*. California, USA: Family Radio.

Chick, Jack. *The Ark*. Archibald, California, USA: Chick Publications, 1976.

Chick, Jack. *Angel of Light*. Archibald, California, USA: Chick Publications.

Chick, Jack. *Big Daddy*. Archibald, California, USA: Chick Publications, 1970.

Chick, Jack. *Primal Man*. Archibald, California, USA: Chick Publications, 2007.

Chick, Jack. *The Battle Cry*. Archibald, California, USA: Chick Publications, 2007.

Chick, Jack. *Sabotage*. Archibald, California, USA: Chick Publications, 1978.

Chittick. D. *The Puzzle of Ancient Man*. Oregon, USA: Creation Compass.

Clayton, Peter. *Chronicle of the Pharaohs*. New York City, USA: Thames and Hudson, 2006.

Comfort, Ray. *Scientific Facts in the Bible*. Bellflower, California: Living Water Publications, 2001.

Cooper, Bill. *After the Flood*. England: New Wine Press, 1995.

Corless, W. *Ancient Man—A Handbook of Puzzling Artifacts*. Maryland, USA: The Source Book Project, 1978.

Custance, A. "The Roots of the Nations" (Internet). USA.

Dillard and Longman. *An Introduction to the Old Testament*. Michigan, USA: Zondervan Publishing, 2006.

Dave, Owner/Publisher, The Coffee Man News, North Jersey, Edition 6/20/13, USA

Douglas and Tenney. *New International Dictionary of the Bible*. Michigan, USA: Zondervan Publishing, 1987.

Eisennman and Wise. *Dead Sea Scrolls Uncovered*. England: Element Ltd., 1992.

Gish, D. *Have You Been Brainwashed?* California, USA: Institute of Creation Research.

Goodman, Watson. *Help from Above*. New Paris, Indiana, USA: World Missionary Press, 1979.

Goodman, Rose. *The Way to God*. New Paris, Indiana, USA: World Missionary Press, 2010.

Finegan, Jack. *Handbook of Biblical Chronology*. New Jersey, USA: Princeton University, 1998.

Halley, H. H. *Halley's Bible Handbook*. Michigan, USA: Zondervan Publishing, 1961.

Hamilton, Victor. *Handbook of the Pentateuch*. Grand Rapids, Michigan, USA: Backer Academic Publishers, 2005.

Hill and Walton. *A Survey of the Old Testament*. Michigan, USA: Zondervan Publishing, 2009.

Hester, H. L. *The Hart for Hebrew History*. Nashville, Tennessee, USA: Broadman Press, 1949.

Hislop, A. *The Two Babylons*. Princeton, New Jersey, USA: Loizeaux Publishers, 2011.

Huse. *The Collapse of Evolution*. Michigan, USA: Baker Book House, 1997.

ICR Impact #349. California, USA: Institute for Creation Research.

Jewish sayings. *The Aggadah*. Jerusalem, Israel: Rossibly the Eshnau Co., 1993.

Kantor, Mattis. *Jewish Time Line Encyclopedia*. New Jersey, USA: Aronson Pub. Co.

KJV. *A Concordance to the Holy Bible*. New York City, USA: American Bible Society.

Kligerman. *Prophecy in the Old Testament*. Michigan, USA: Zondervan Publishing, 1957.

Kuiper, B. *The Church in History*. Ontario, Canada: Eerdmans Publishing, 1988.

Lambert, Dolphin. "Tower of Babel and Confusion of Languages" (Internet). USA.

Lesten, Stephen. *The Bible in World History*. Uhrichsville, Ohio, USA: Barbour Publishing, Inc., 2011.

Lubenov, M. *Bones of Contention*. CSI Publishers, 1992.

Macmillan. *Encyclopedia Judaica*. Jerusalem, Israel: Keter Co.

Mader, Sylvia. *Inquiry into Life*. USA: McGraw-Hill Publishers, 2007.

Marks, Pat. *Someone's Making a Monkey Out of You*. Arkansas, USA: Master Books.

McGee, J. V. *Through the Bible—Genesis*. Thomas Nelson Publishers.

Miller, Stephen. *The Complete Guide to the Bible*. Uhrichsville, Ohio, USA: Barbour Publishing, Inc., 2007.

Montgomery, John. *The Quest for Noah's Ark*. Minnesota, USA: Bethany Fellowship, 1972.

Morris, Henry. *Evolution and the Modern Christians*. Michigan, USA: Baker Book House.

Morris, Henry. *Scientific Creationism*. El Cajon, California, USA: Master Books, 1974.

Morris, John. *The Young Earth*. California, USA: JCR Institute for Creation Research.

Nissen, Henri, Noah's Ark, Vision Publishing. VA, USA.

Outler, Albert. *The Works of John Wesley*. Nashville, Tennessee, USA: Abington Press, 1989.

Richards, L. *The Smart Guide to the Bible*. Thomas Nelson Publishers.

Riss, R. *Christian Evidences* (Internet). New Jersey, USA: Pillar Christian College.

Riss, R. *Time Line for the Old Testament*. Zarephath, New Jersey, USA: Pillar Christian College.

Segraves, K. *The Great Dinosaur Mistake*. California, USA: Bata Books.

Spielvogel, J. *Western Civilization*. USA: West Publishing Co.

Swaggart, James. *Swaggart Study Bible KJV*. Louisiana, USA: Swaggart Evangelical Assoc.

Tyndale and Coverdale. *1611 King James Bible*. Nashville, Tennessee, USA: Nelson Publishers.

Waite, D. A. *Defending the King James Bible*. New Jersey, USA: The Old Paths Publications, Inc., 1998.

Walker, Tas. "Has the Garden of Eden Been Found?" (Internet). USA.

Walton, J. *Charts of the Old Testament*. Michigan, USA: Zondervan Publishing.

Ward. D. S. "The Adams Family" (Internet). USA.

Water, Mark. *Genesis Made Easy*. Peabody, Massachusetts, USA: Henderson Publishers, 2002.

Wilkerson, Dave. "Tearing Down Altars" (sermon). Times Square Church, New York City, USA.

Wilson, Ian. *Before the Flood*. New York, USA: St. Martin's Press, 2002.

Young, R. *Analytical Concordance to the Bible*. New York City, USA: Funk and Wagnalls, 1984.

Youngblood, R. *New International Bible Notes*. Michigan, USA: Zondervan Publishing.

Information provided by Rev. M. Bailston, Messengers of the New Covenant in New Jersey.

Information provided by Professor. Haag of Somerset Christian College, Zarephath, New Jersey.

Information provided by Prof. R. Riss of Somerset Christian College, Zarephath, New Jersey.

Information provided by Richard Cannarella of Evangelism Ministries, New Jersey and South Carolina, USA.

Information provided by Rabbi Teitz of the Jewish Education Center, Elizabeth, New Jersey.

Information provided by the Southwest Institute of Biblical and Theological Studies in New Mexico.

Information gathered from science and history programs on television.

Note: Any information in this history book is based upon the authorized 1611 King James Bible, the most accurate and literal translation we have available today.

LETTERS OF ENDORSEMENT

May 25, 2013

Mr. Bob Koerner
32 Amy Ct.
Brick, NJ 08724

RE: Review of "Exploring Genesis"

"Exploring Genesis" commentary by Mr. Bob Koerner is both interesting and inviting in bringing insight to this great book of the beginnings.

By Koener's uncomplicated commentary, he shows readers how to gain understanding with this unassuming, clear teaching. One can gain confidence in navigating Genesis and then be able to practically enlighten others about the context. This commentary contains helpful research, both biblical and practical. What he is disclosing here is backed by Scripture and knowledge of God's Word.

By sharing this knowledge, Koener facilitates assistance and a step-by-step guide into practical perspectives in solving biblical ambiguities and lays a foundation that the reader can continue to build upon.

I recommend the use of this commentary as a guide to a deeper understanding of Genesis. My prayer is that this commentary would be exposed in a way that would bear much fruit for God's kingdom.

Respectfully submitted,

Joseph Korn
Pastor

1669 North Bay Avenue Toms River, New Jersey 08753
PH: 732-244-5580

Love Never Fails

John DiGiamberardino
Pastor

Matthew Kay
Director of
Youth Ministries

Barry Glickman
Christian School Principal

Barbara Estelle
Director of Music
Organist

Saint Paul's Church
A United Methodist Congregation
714 Herbertsville Road,
Brick, New Jersey 08724
(732)458-2080 Church (732)
458-2004 Christian School

January 2013

To Whom It May Concern,

I am writing in support of the work written by Mr. Robert Koerner, entitled, **Exploring Genesis**. After spending a great amount of time reading this work, I can clearly recognize the intense research done for this project. For the person who wants to learn about the origins of humanity this work is essential.

Mr. Koerner included valuable information in the chapter titled "Table of Nations." I was honored that Mr. Koerner would ask me to read his work and I sincerely endorse its publication.

John DiGiamberardino
Pastor: St. Paul's United
Methodist Church.

Our Purpose

"***Praise*** God through worship, ***grow*** as disciples through study,
share our faith through testimony, and
serve others through ministry."

Letter of Recommendation

September 18, 2008 A.D.

DEAR READER,

I have known Mr. Bob Koerner, the author of "Exploring Genesis," since the early 1980s when we rode the train together every day from Cranford to Newark, New Jersey. We studied the Bible along the way. We had some glorious times together, discovering things about the Lord. I was a brand-new Christian, and Bob helped me understand the things of the Lord. I have never met anyone who loves the Word of God more than Bob. He encouraged me to be more vocal in my Christian ministry. He also inspired me to find out the meanings and the importance of the Hebrew names God gave to the individuals in Scripture. Bob had shown me that the names of the people and places in scripture were a story within themselves. I have used Bob's idea of "the story within the story" many times in my own ministry. I'm glad Bob took the time to record these kinds of things for others to use.

In those days, Bob and I started the street evangelism ministry called EvangelArm Ministries. We would take the Word to the street comers in Manhattan (NYC) and Westfield, New Jersey. Many people passing by us heard the gospel. Some came to Christ. I can still hear Bob's voice ringing out, "Listen, you people." He has always had a desire for people to hear what he had to say about our Lord, Jesus Christ

I have read "Exploring Genesis," Bob's first book, and find it extremely interesting. It is packed with the kinds of details I need when I do my own research for my preaching. These facts and findings should help every student of the book of Genesis to put things in their respective order. With the "wild" evolutionists theories and the "new morality" mentality surrounding everything we Christians attempt to do, we need to have these kinds of true facts about man's origins, sin (and there is such a thing as sin), faith, and salvation readily at hand.

I know you will be blessed as you read "Exploring Genesis." Follow up on the references that Bob has provided for more details regarding our Christian faith. Accept Bob's challenge and be prepared to receive more insight as you yourself study the Word of God.

Richard A. Cannarella, Director
EvangelArm Ministries
P.O. Box 3943
Anderson SC 29622
richword@charter.net

Rev. Donald Hyer, D. Min
OCEAN SCHOOL OF MINISTRY. 1133 E. COUNTY LINE RD, LAKEWOOD, NJ 08701

dhyer@calvarylighthouse org

TEL 732-363-8009

February 6, 2013
Mr. Robert Koerner
32 Amy Court
Brick, NJ 08724

Dear Mr. Koerner:

It is apparent that a great deal of time and effort has gone into the preparation of your study, "Exploring Genesis." Your point of view is set forth very clearly, and, while the material is not original (beware the "original" in biblical studies: the ancients have stolen our most brilliant ideas, and our "original" is usually heretical), it is a fairly concise summary of [the] fundamental teaching of this topic.

Its nature is polemical, that is, the declaration of this point of view, with attempted destruction of opposing views rather than apologetic, bringing forth a superior vision that is better than others, showing their strong and weak points and leading the reader to his or her conclusion.

My opinion is that the study is publishable, but its marketability is questionable. One has to have quite a wide base of potential purchasers or spend a considerable sum for others to market it in order to have a return to you.

Respectfully,

Donald Hyer

July 4, 2010

Re: Genesis

Where did we come from? Were we just a biological accident or part of a much grander design? How can we trace the origin of the nations of the world? Why do we wear clothing? One book has the answers: Genesis.

Through careful research, Bob has made the answers to complex questions simple and understandable. Bob's book is an excellent resource for serious students as well as casual readers. In its pages, the reader will discover the lies society has come to accept as facts, be able to replace it with truth, and then defend it

The analysis contained in each chapter greatly compliments the biblical text and will motivate the reader to go back to Genesis again and again. I happily recommend it!

Phil Quagliariello, Elder
Trinity Bible Church
Allenwood, NJ

1131 Fellowship Road
Basking Ridge NJ 07920
908 604 8377
frair@sprynet.com
04 Ah 04

Mr. Robert P. Koerner
PO Box 1371
Elizabeth NJ 07207

Dear Rob,

Thank you for sharing your book with me. I think that the manuscript is beautifully prepared and very interesting reading. You brought out some information of which I had not been aware, especially regarding the Bible. It is clear that a lot of work has been invested in producing your manuscript.

I am somewhat uncertain about what to recommend regarding publication because the writing primarily has a historical perspective rather than scientific, which, as you know, is my field.

You had asked about doctors Gish and Morris, who are at the Institute for Creation Research in California. I think that they may not be the best referees for the manuscript because of the scientific emphases in their training, research and writing. I expect, rather, that biblical historians would be better evaluators.

May God continue to bless in your life, Rob. Thank you for your friendship.

Yours in Christ,

Wayne Frair

PS. I am returning the manuscript separately in a box.

December 12, 2005

Rev. Dr. Brady Mc Daniels
1244 West Farms Road
Howell, NJ 07731

Re: Genesis Book Review, Author Robert Koerner

The reading of Genesis was a very interesting read. Mr. Koerner did a very good job of researching his subject. It was also very interesting that be categorized his topics in a very revealing way, particularly the third (3) chapter.

I found his work to be intelligent, meaningful and understandable. I would recommend this reading for anyone interested in the origin of Genesis.

Respectfully,

Rev. Dr Brady McDaniels, MFT
Director of Chaplaincy
Clinical Manager Family Matters InFocus

Cc: Mr. Robert Koerner

Ms. Susan Dougherty
SD Secretarial Service
250 W. 2nd Avenue
Roselle, NJ 07203

September 2, 2009

TO: Robert P. Koerner

RE: Review of "Exploring Genesis"
(Author, Robert P. Koerner)

"EXPLORING GENESIS" is an excellent, well-researched book, containing much interesting material about the book of Genesis. It is presented in a well-organized and relatively concise manner as well.

Mr. Koemer's link between the Tower of Babel and the Twin Towers of NYC make his book especially relevant to our modern day world.

"All scripture is given by Inspiration of God, and is profitable for doctrine, for reproof, for correction, for Instruction in righteousness" (2 Timothy 3:16). Mr. Koerner's research has certainly sought to fulfill this purpose.

The material will be useful for pastors, students and lay people alike as a Bible study aid.

It was a real privilege to be involved in the editing and proofing of this book—a wonderful, enlightening and enriching experience.

It has also been good to know Mr. Koerner on a personal level as a former neighbor and friend. His love for his Lord and Savior, Jesus Christ, is a true inspiration. He attended a Bible study in our home for several years and made many worthwhile contributions to our biblical discussions based on his massive historical knowledge of the Bible.

"EXPLORING GENESIS" is a worthwhile experience in the expansion of biblical knowledge and understanding of the book of Genesis.

I highly recommend it as a part of any library, classroom or Bible study.

Respectfully,

Susan Dougherty, Owner and Operator of SD Secretarial Service

June 24, 2009

Mr. Bob. Koerner
32 Amy Ct
Brick, NJ 08724

Dear Mr. Bob Koerner,

Thank you so much for sending Jews for Jesus your commentary "Exploring Genesis." We truly appreciate you thinking of us by sharing your hard work.

Obviously, you have spent a great deal of time and effort in the research and production of this manuscript

I pray God's blessings on you as you continue to share this wonderful project with others. Please continue to travel the road God has so graciously chosen for you.

My prayers are with you.

In Him,

Susan Perlman
Associate Executive Director
Jews for Jesus
60 Haight Street
San Francisco, CA 94102

60 Haight Street. San Francisco. CA 94102-5895
e-mail: jfj@jewsforjesus.org | web: jewsforjesus.org | 415.864.2600

Exploring Genesis with Conviction: A Review of Bob Harty Koerner's Work

Bob Harty Koerner's Exploring the Book of Genesis serves as an excellent introduction to the foundational questions raised by the Genesis narratives, particularly in an age of skepticism about the Bible's historical reliability. From the outset, Koerner's love for Scripture and deep conviction that the Bible, especially Genesis, offers life-giving truths shine through.

The book introduces readers to critical scholarly debates surrounding Genesis, with particular attention to the first eleven chapters. Koerner defends a traditional interpretation of the text, arguing for a young earth, a six-day creation, the historical reality of Adam and Eve as uniquely created individuals, and the historicity of Noah's flood. These positions, often dismissed by non-Christians, are also frequently accepted uncritically by Christians who adopt a "God said it, I believe it, that settles it" mindset, without asking, "Why do I believe this?"

Koerner challenges this superficial approach by providing extensive research and evidence to support his views. He demonstrates that the traditional grammatical-historical interpretation of Genesis is not only reasonable but also offers a solid foundation for a robust biblical worldview.

This book is a valuable resource for anyone grappling with questions about Genesis in a skeptical world. Whether you are a believer seeking to deepen your understanding or a skeptic exploring the text's claims, Koerner's thoughtful analysis and clear articulation will leave you better equipped to engage with these critical issues.

Hope this is helpful
Rev. Dr. William A. Meyer
Pastor of Congregational Care, True Life Church

This book is quick read with a lot of documented information. A valuable resource for S.S. teachers and all serious Bible students. The book of Genesis is foundational to all of Sacred Scripture.

Rev. Paul A Tye. Ordained minister with the A.G. since 1967.

Dear reader,

I really enjoyed reading *Exploring the Book of Genesis* written by Bob Koerner. What an excellent resource put together with scripture and experts on the subject of the genesis of all creation. I believe this book would be a great resource for new believers or for curious readers looking for truth.

Thank you, Bob, for all the research and time you put into this book. I'm looking forward to reading the second edition. God bless everyone. May this book help you find the truth of God's plan from the beginning.

Sincerely yours,
Frank Martinez

Dear reader,

St. Augustine famously said, "Our heart is restless until it rests in you, Lord." This book will help you know God and to know God is to Love God. You need not agree with all precepts but will be challenged to think or rethink…or if nothing else, do more research. This book is an easy read with nuggets of wisdom and humor. The author is someone who clearly places all trust in God and so has written for all humanity so as to change hearts and minds for the betterment of all mankind.

Sincerely,
Philip Mylod, Esq.

This book is a quick read with a lot of documentation information. A valuable resource for SS teachers and all serious Bible students. The book of Genesis is foundational to all of sacred scripture.

Rev. Paul A. Tye, ordained minister with the AG since 1967

ABOUT THE AUTHOR

At the time of the researching of this book (2002), Bob Harty Koerner was a history student at Somerset Christian College in Zarephath, New Jersey. His unusual nickname (Conrail) comes from the fact that he is a railroad enthusiast. Bob is one of the founding fathers of Evangelarm Ministries. He was also a member of the Wildlife Conservation Society and Ocean County Historical Society, a Christian stand-up comedian, a musician, a classical concert flutist, and a licensed New York City tour guide. Since the year AD 2002, after the first draft of this book, Bob has graduated with honors from Freedom Bible College in Rodgers, Arkansas. Bob possesses an extraordinary knowledge of the Old Testament and is regarded by some local scholars as an authority on the Bible, especially on the book of Genesis (refer to References). Bob is a U.S. Army Veteran. Bob is ready and available for speaking engagements at churches and colleges. He is an astute individual and knowledgeable debater and welcomes any positive or negative commentary regarding this book. This author will openly debate any topic of interest relating to this book. Write to PO Box 1817, Brick, New Jersey 08724.

Bob Harty Koerner